TRUE WORSHIPPER'S GUIDE TO HIS PRESENCE

ENTERING INTO THE HOLY OF HOLIES

Bishop Dr. Emmanuel D. Apau Jr.

TRUE WORSHIPPER'S GUIDE TO HIS PRESENCE
ENTERING INTO THE HOLY OF HOLIES

ISBN: 978 – 9988 – 2 – 6898 – 5

Cover Design: Graceland Products & Services

Editors: Alfreda S. Grace, Bishop Dr. Emmanuel D. Apau Jr.

For further enquiries, contact the author at:
P. O. Box 951. Akim Oda, E/R. Ghana
Email: worldlightbishop@gmail.com

DEDICATION

This book is dedicated to all my spiritual children in the United States who have shown love, care, and support, and have dedicated their time and resources. I love you all. May the Lord God help you live to enjoy the fruit of your labor.

To all who have passed through my hands in the teachings of our Lord Jesus Christ and all who are waiting for His glorious return, His second coming, and the endless kingdom to come.

To all true followers of Jesus Christ.

ACKNOWLEDGEMENT

I would like to acknowledge all the true worshippers who have dedicated their lives unto the service of our Lord Jesus Christ.

I thank my Music director, Mr. Martin for all his support and encouragement. To all my brothers and sisters, both in the Lord and biologically, for their wonderful love and support in all my life-endeavors. Brethren, I am very grateful for you. You have helped me to actualize my dreams and ambitions.

I am grateful to the Dean and Vice President of New Life Bible College and Seminary, Dr. Sandy Haga, who played a supportive role in my life when I was a student in the seminary.

To my wife, Angela G. Akyea, thank you for standing by my side when things were difficult and, also, for your hard work in bringing these books into reality. You are the best wife. Sweetheart, may God richly bless you. To my parents, Mr. Stephen Oyinka Apau and Mrs. Mercy Darkwa Apau, thanks for your great love for me.

To all who have supported this project, both financially and spiritually, I am very grateful for you. Thank you for your time, prayers, love, hospitality, financial assistance and various other forms of support. May God richly bless you all.

SPECIAL THANKS

Special thanks to my Heavenly Father, God Almighty, for His help and wisdom to put this book together.

CONTENTS

INTRODUCTION

Praise and worship take us into the presence of God. When we praise God in the midst of seemingly negative situations, we are affirming our faith in Him. Praise, thanksgiving, and worship are powerful weapons for the believer and it is the desire of the Lord that we worship Him with one mind and in unity. The devil fears and simply cannot stand the unity of the saints in the praise and worship of the Lord.

Romans 15.5-6(KJV)Now the God of patience and consolation grant you to be likeminded one toward another according to Christ Jesus: {according to: or, after the example of} That ye may with one mind and one mouth glorify God, even the Father of our Lord Jesus Christ.

Praise and worship destroys the strongholds of Satan and crushes all his attacks:

Acts 16:16-34(KJV) "And it came to pass, as we went to prayer, a certain damsel possessed with a spirit of divination met us, which brought her masters much gain by soothsaying: {of divination: or, of Python} 17 The same followed Paul and us, and cried, saying, These men are the servants of the most high God, which shew unto us the way of salvation. 18 And this did she many days. But Paul, being grieved, turned and said to the spirit, I command thee in the name of Jesus Christ to come out of her. And he came out the same hour. 19 And when her masters saw that the hope of their gains was gone, they caught Paul and Silas, and drew them into the marketplace unto the rulers, {marketplace: or, court} 20 And brought them to the magistrates, saying, These men, being Jews, do exceedingly trouble our city, 21 And teach customs, which are not lawful for us to receive, neither to observe, being Romans. 22 And the multitude rose up together against them: and the magistrates rent off their clothes, and commanded to beat them. 23 And when they had laid many stripes upon them, they cast them into prison, charging the jailor to keep them safely: 24 Who, having received such a charge, thrust them into the inner prison, and made their feet fast in the stocks. 25 And at midnight Paul and Silas prayed, and sang praises unto God: and the prisoners heard them. 26 And suddenly there was a great earthquake, so that the foundations of the prison were shaken: and immediately all the doors were opened, and every one's bands were loosed. 27 And the keeper of the prison awaking out of his sleep, and seeing the prison doors open, he drew out his sword, and would have killed himself, supposing that the prisoners had been fled. 28 But Paul cried with a loud voice, saying, Do thyself no harm: for we are all here. 29 Then he called for a light, and sprang in, and came trembling, and fell down before Paul and Silas, 30 And brought them out, and said, Sirs, what must I do to be saved? 31 And they said, Believe on the Lord Jesus Christ, and thou shalt be saved, and thy house. 32 And they spake unto him the word of the Lord, and to all that were in his house. 33 And he took them the same hour of the night, and washed their stripes; and was baptized, he and all his, straightway. 34 And when he had brought them into his house, he set meat before them, and rejoiced, believing in God with all his house."

Psalm 149.1-9(KJV) *" Praise ye the LORD. Sing unto the LORD a new song, and his praise in the congregation of saints. {Praise...: Heb. Hallelujah} 2 Let Israel rejoice in him that made him: let the children of Zion be joyful in their King. {in him...: Heb. in his Makers} 3 Let them praise his name in the dance: let them sing praises unto him with the timbrel and harp. {in...: or, with the pipe} 4 For the LORD taketh pleasure in his people: he will beautify the meek with salvation. 5 Let the saints be joyful in glory: let them sing aloud upon their beds.6 Let the high praises of God be in their mouth, and a twoedged sword in their hand; {mouth: Heb. throat} 7 To execute vengeance upon the heathen,* *and punishments upon the people; 8 To bind their kings with chains, and their nobles with fetters of iron; 9 To execute upon them the judgment written: this honour have all his saints. Praise ye the LORD."*

True praise and worship begins in the Outer Court, moves to the Holy Place and ends in the Holy of Holies where communion between divinity and humanity takes place. There are some who are Outer Court worshippers (those who worship in the flesh), while others are Holy Place Worshippers (those who worship in the soul-realm, the place of desire); yet, they never reach the Holy of Holies (the place of communion with God) due to a lack of preparation, seriousness, holiness and much more. The truth of the matter is that it is the heart desire of the Lord for His children to enter through His gates and come into His presence.

***Psalm 100.1-5(KJV)** "A Psalm of praise. Make a joyful noise unto the LORD, all ye lands. {praise: or, thanksgiving} {all...: Heb. all the earth} Serve the LORD with gladness: come before his presence with singing. Know ye that the LORD he is God: it is he that hath made us, and not we ourselves; we are his people, and the sheep of his pasture. {and not...: or, and his we are} Enter into his gates with thanksgiving, and into his courts with praise: be thankful unto him, and bless his name. For the LORD is good; his mercy is everlasting; and his truth endureth to all generations. {to all...: Heb. to generation and generation}"*

There are two types of ministrations that we often see in many godly gatherings; that is, the ministration of the Word and ministration through songs. These are the most powerful vehicles that cause the Lord to move strongly and allow His presence or glory to be experienced in any godly institution or gathering. The ministration of the Word is where we gather at the feet of the Lord to hear His word and voice through His faithful ministers from the fivefold ministries (Apostolic, Prophetic, Evangelistic, Pastoral, and Teaching) so that the body of Christ will reach the unity of faith and come to a point of maturity, lacking nothing.

Song ministration sessions are periods where vocalists and instrumentalists, gifted by God with the Spirit of music, lead the church or the congregation by ministering through songs before the Lord and unto our King, Jesus. We minister before the Lord through praise, worship, solos, etc. depending on the gathering, occasion, timing and what we want to say about and unto our God. Praise excites you before the Lord, but worship humbles you before Him.

CHAPTER ONE

WHAT IS PRAISE AND WORSHIP?

Praise and worship are very essential in our service to the Lord and King. Praise makes you joyous and active and it excites you before the King, but worship breaks or humbles you before the King. If this is so, then we must understand the differences between praise and worship, and we must know some of the important roles they play in our Christian walk.

Praise

Praise is the act of praising God; it is the act of singing songs of praise to Him and about Him. Praise makes us excited before the Lord. God delights in praise and dwells among us through our praise. Spiritually, true praise chairs or enthrones the Lord and allows Him to dwell among His congregation. Whenever praise ascends from the congregation, the glory of the Lord comes down.

Psalm22.3 (KJV) But thou art holy, O thou that inhabitest the praises of Israel.

Psalm 22.3 (NET) You are holy; you sit as king receiving the praises of Israel.

It is recommended for all to praise God and to sing praises unto His name.

Psalm 135(KJV) "1Praise ye the LORD. Praise ye the name of the LORD; praise him, O ye servants of the LORD. 2 Ye that stand in the house of the LORD, in the courts of the house of our God, 3 Praise the LORD;

for the LORD is good: sing praises unto his name; for it is pleasant. 4 For the LORD hath chosen Jacob unto himself, and Israel for his peculiar treasure."5 For I know that the LORD is great, and that our Lord is above all gods. 6 Whatsoever the LORD pleased, that did he in heaven, and in earth, in the seas, and all deep places

Psalm117.1-2 *O praise the LORD, all ye nations: praise him, all ye people. 2 For his merciful kindness is great toward us: and the truth of the LORD endureth for ever. Praise ye the LORD.*

Praise excites you before the King.

Psalm 45.15-17 *"With gladness and rejoicing shall they be brought: they shall enter into the king's palace. 16Instead of thy fathers shall be thy children, whom thou mayest make princes in all the earth. 17 I will make thy name to be remembered in all generations: therefore shall the people praise thee forever and ever"*

Worship

Worship is the act of expressing gratitude and showing reverence to God (Elohim), the highest deity (Divinity) and the Supreme Being, by telling Him who He is in every aspect of your life. Worship goes beyond thanksgiving, although it does begin with giving thanks. The reason is that we thank God for what He has done, but we worship Him for who He is. In other words, the true worshipper does not worship the Lord only because of the things He has done, but for who He is; His nature, attributes, etc.

__Psalm 96.7-9__ "Give unto the LORD, O ye kindreds of the people, give unto the LORD glory and strength. 8Give unto the LORD the glory due unto his name: bring an offering, and come into his courts. {due...: Heb. of his name} 9O worship the LORD in the beauty of holiness: fear before him, all the earth. {in the...: or, in the glorious sanctuary"

__Psalm 138:1-5__ "1 <<A Psalm of David. >> I will praise thee with my whole heart: before the gods will I sing praise unto thee. 2 I will worship toward thy holy temple, and praise thy name for thy lovingkindness and for thy truth: for thou hast magnified thy word above all thy name. 3 In the day when I cried thou answeredst me, and strengthenedst me with strength in my soul. 4 All the kings of the earth shall praise thee, O LORD, when they hear the words of thy mouth. 5 Yea, they shall sing in the ways of the LORD: for great is the glory of the LORD."

True worship goes behind the veil or curtains, into the Holy of Holies. In the Outer Court, the flesh cries out in worship. In the Holy Place, we surrender our will, intellect, emotion, and desires to the Lord. The Holy of Holies is where true communion takes place. Worship, is a way of life. It is a lifestyle and that is why our Lord said, in His word and through the Apostle Paul, that we must present our bodies as a living sacrifice, holy and acceptable unto the Lord.

__Romans 12.1-2(KJV)__ 1 I beseech you therefore, brethren, by the mercies of God, that ye present your bodies a living sacrifice, holy, acceptable unto God, which is your reasonable service. 2 And be not conformed to this world: but be ye transformed by the renewing of your mind, that ye may prove what *is that good, and acceptable, and perfect, will of God.*

Worship is a humble, yet active, way of reverencing God and it must become our way of life. Most importantly, we must understand that true praise and worship is spiritual, and since we dwell in a physical body, we must first learn how to honor the Lord with our bodies. If not, our worship cannot be accepted and is vain. Before we can please the Lord in the Spirit in our praise and worship sessions and have an encounter with Lord, we must first learn how to give ourselves fully unto God as a living sacrifice, holy and acceptable. We must give Him true worship and everything He requires of us.

Worship is also an act of reverencing and paying homage to God:

> ***Ex 20:3-6(KJV)*** *"Thou shalt have no other gods before me. 4Thou shalt not make unto thee any graven image, or any likeness of anything that is in heaven above, or that is in the earth beneath, or that is in the water under the earth: 5Thou shalt not bow down thyself to them, nor serve them: for I the LORD thy God am a jealous God, visiting the iniquity of the fathers upon the children unto the third and fourth generation of them that hate me; 6And shewing mercy unto thousands of them that love me, and keep my commandments".*

We can offer praise and worship to the Lord in various places and settings. Also, our worship and praise to the Lord must be offered in a specific way that is prescribed by the Lord. The sad fact is that many of the things that actually cause our worship to reach God's standard, such as prayer, the word, the understand of the blood and the cross of Jesus Christ, are the very things that so-called worshippers of today are not interested in. This is one of the main reasons why much of the worship that is offered in many churches today is unacceptable to God and or is often shallow.

- Worship and praise may be given in a temple:

  Jeremiah 26:2 "Thus saith the LORD; Stand in the court of the LORD'S house, and speak unto all the cities of Judah, which come to worship in the LORD'S house, all the words that I command thee to speak unto them; diminish not a word"

  Luke 24:50-53 "And he led them out as far as to Bethany, and he lifted up his hands, and blessed them. 51 And it came to pass, while he blessed them, he was parted from them, and carried up into heaven. 52 And they worshipped him, and returned to Jerusalem with great joy:53 And were continually in the temple, praising and blessing God. Amen."

- Worship and praise may be done in our homes:

  Acts 5:42 "And daily in the temple, and in every house, they ceased not to teach and preach Jesus Christ"

  Rom 16:5 "Likewise greet the church that is in their house. Salute my well beloved Epaenetus, who is the first fruits of Achaia unto Christ"

- Worship and praise must be offered out of true devotion unto the Lord:

  Hebrew 10:22-25 "Let us draw near with a true heart in full assurance of faith, having our hearts sprinkled from an evil conscience, and our bodies washed with pure water. 23 Let us hold fast the profession of our faith without wavering; (for he is faithful that promised;) 24 And let us consider one another to provoke unto love and to good works: 25 Not forsaking the assembling of ourselves together, as the manner of some is; but exhorting one another: and so much the more, as ye see the day approaching".

- Praise and worship to God must come from a willing heart:

Proverbs 8:33-36 (KJV) *Hear instruction, and be wise, and refuse it not. 34 Blessed is the man that heareth me, watching daily at my gates, waiting at the posts of my doors. 35For whoso findeth me findeth life, and shall obtain favour of the LORD. {obtain: Heb. bring forth} 36But he that sinneth against me wrongeth his own soul: all they that hate me love death.)*

- Worship and praise must be offered in accordance with the divine rules:

1 Corinth 11:1-34 (KJV) *1 Be ye followers of me, even as I also am of Christ. 2Now I praise you, brethren, that ye remember me in all things, and keep the ordinances, as I delivered them to you. {ordinances: or, traditions} 3 But I would have you know, that the head of every man is Christ; and the head of the woman is the man; and the head of Christ is God. 4Every man praying or prophesying, having his head covered, dishonoureth his head. 5But every woman that prayeth or prophesieth with her head uncovered dishonoureth her head: for that is even all one as if she were shaven. 6For if the woman* *be not covered, let her also be shorn: but if it be a shame for a woman to be shorn or shaven, let her be covered. 7For a man indeed ought not to cover his head, forasmuch as he is the image and glory of God: but the woman is the glory of the man. 8For the man is not of the woman; but the woman of the man. 9 Neither was the man created for the woman; but the woman for the man. 10For this cause ought the woman to have power on her head because of the angels. {power: that is a covering in sign that she is under the power of her husband} 11Nevertheless neither is the man without the woman, neither the woman without the man, in the Lord. 12For as the woman is of the man, even so is the man also by the woman; but all things of God. 13Judge in yourselves: is it comely that a woman pray unto God uncovered? 14Doth not even nature itself teach you, that, if a man have long hair, it is a shame unto him? 15But if a woman have long hair, it is a glory to her: for her hair is given her for a covering. {covering: or, veil} 16But if any man seem to be contentious, we have no such custom, neither the churches of God.17 Now in this that I declare unto you I praise you not, that ye come together not for the better, but for the worse. 18 For first of all, when ye come together in the church, I hear that there be divisions among you; and I partly believe it. {divisions: or, schisms} 19 For there must be also heresies among you, that they which are approved may be made manifest among you. {heresies: or, sects} 20 When ye come together therefore into one place, this is not to eat the Lord's supper. {this...: or, ye cannot eat} 21 For in eating every one taketh before other his own supper: and one is hungry, and another is drunken. 22 What? have ye not houses to eat and to drink in? or despise ye the church of God, and shame them that have not? What shall I say to you? shall I praise you in this? I praise you not. {have not: or, are poor?} 23 For I have received of the Lord that which also I delivered unto you, That the Lord Jesus the same night in which he was betrayed took bread: 24 And when he had given thanks, he brake it, and said, Take, eat: this is my body, which is broken for you: this do in remembrance of me. {in...: or, for a remembrance} 25 After the same manner also he took the cup, when he had supped, saying, This cup is the new testament in my blood: this do ye, as oft as ye drink it, in remembrance of me. 26 For as often as ye eat this bread, and drink this cup, ye do shew the Lord's death till he come. {ye do...: or, shew ye} 27 Wherefore whosoever shall eat this bread, and drink this cup of the Lord, unworthily, shall be guilty of the body and blood of the Lord. 28 But let a man examine himself, and so let him eat of that bread, and drink of that cup. 29 For he that eateth and drinketh unworthily, eateth and drinketh damnation to himself, not discerning the Lord's body. {damnation: or, judgment} 30 For this cause many are weak and sickly among you, and many sleep. 31 For if we would judge ourselves, we should not be judged. 32 But when we are judged, we are chastened of the Lord, that we should not be condemned with the world. 33 Wherefore, my brethren, when ye come together to eat, tarry one for another. 34 And if any man hunger, let him eat at home; that ye come not together unto condemnation. And the rest will I set in order when I come. {condemnation: or, judgment}).*

True worship and praise are achieved through prayer:

***1 Thessalonians 3:10(KJV)** Night and day praying exceedingly that we might see your face, and might perfect that which is lacking in your faith?.*

True worship and praise are also achieved through the singing of psalms and hymns:

***Ephesians 5:18-20** And be not drunk with wine, wherein is excess; but be filled with the Spirit; 19 Speaking to yourselves in psalms and hymns and spiritual songs, singing and making melody in your heart to the Lord; 20 Giving thanks always for all things unto God and the Father in the name of our Lord Jesus Christ,*

True worship and praise can be achieved with music. Music is just one of the facets of our worship and praise. There are various components and ways by which we offer true worship and praise. Yet, music is one of the ways through which we worship and praise God; and worshippers must learn how to use music appropriately to glorify and honor Him.

***Ps 81:1-3** <<To the chief Musician upon Gittith, A Psalm of Asaph. >> Sing aloud unto God our strength: make a joyful noise unto the God of Jacob. {of Asaph: or, for Asaph} 2 Take a psalm, and bring hither the timbrel, the pleasant harp with the psaltery. 3 Blow up the trumpet in the new moon, in the time appointed, on our solemn feast day.*

Worship and praise can be achieved through the preaching of the gospel:

Although our lifestyles must serve as our worship unto the Lord, we must also set a specific time apart to worship God. That is also very important and cannot be neglected.

CHAPTER TWO

THE LORD DESIRES TRUE WORSHIPPERS

Who is a true worshipper?

True worshippers are people who have been prepared and trained to give praise and worship unto the Lord through their actions, words, and music, etc., as it has been prescribed by the word of God. Their primary objective and goal is to prepare God's people in every way to help them to get into God's presence through sound biblical teachings and doctrines of holiness, righteousness, and the knowledge about the blood of the Lamb, and through all kinds of spiritual songs. True worshippers aim to create an atmosphere for the King of Glory through biblical instruments, hymns, spiritual songs, and the right presentation of the Word so that the presence of God will dwell in the gathering of His people. They aim to move the body of Christ from the Outer Court and the Holy Place into the Holy of Holies, where communion with God takes place; where deep calls for deep, evil cannot enter, and everything is possible, except sin. For our Lord God and Master, Yahweh, to dwell amongst His people, there must be true worshippers who will worship in the Spirit and in truth. There must be spiritual Levites, ordained and trained by the Lord, to offer God the right kind of praise and worship. There must be the proper use of instrumentation, as prescribed by God, to create a divine atmosphere for God's presence to descend. Proper presentation of worship and praise must also be orchestrated to cause the people to join together and magnify the Lord. Remember that it takes true worshippers to worship in spirit and in truth. If you want to get to the King, you must worship in the Holy Ghost and dwell in the secret place, the Holy of Holies (Psalm 91). You must be a true worshipper.

Scriptural basis:

> ***Psalm 91.1-2*** He that dwelleth in the secret place of the most High shall abide under the shadow of the Almighty. I will say of the Lord, He is my refuge and my fortress: my God; in him will I trust.

> ***John 4.23*** *But a time is coming and has now come when the true worshipers will worship the Father in spirit and in truth, for the Father is seeking such as these to worship Him24God is a Spirit: and they that worship him must worship him in spirit and in truth.*

> ***Psalm 50.13-14*** *"Shall I eat the flesh of bulls or drink the blood of male goats? 14"Offer to God a sacrifice of thanksgiving And pay your vows to the Most High;*

> ***Hebrews10.19-22*** *Therefore brothers, having confidence for entering the holy places by the blood of Jesus, 20by a new and living way, which He dedicated for us through the veil that is His flesh, 21and having a great priest over the house of God, 22we should draw near with a sincere heart, in full assurance of faith, our hearts having been sprinkled clean from an evil conscience and our body having been washed with pure water;*

> ***Psalm100. 4*** *Enter His gates with thanksgiving And His courts with praise. Give thanks to Him, bless His*

name. 5For the LORD is good; His lovingkindness is everlasting And His faithfulness to all generations.

***2Ch 5:11-14** And it came to pass, when the priests were come out of the holy place: (for all the priests that were present were sanctified, and did not then wait by course: (12) Also the Levites which were the singers, all of them of Asaph, of Heman, of Jeduthun, with their sons and their brethren, being arrayed in white linen, having cymbals and psalteries and harps, stood at the east end of the altar, and with them an hundred and twenty priests sounding with trumpets:) (13) It came even to pass, as the trumpeters and singers were as one, to make one sound to be heard in praising and thanking the LORD; and when they lifted up their voice with the trumpets and cymbals and instruments of musick, and praised the LORD, saying, For he is good; for his mercy endureth for ever: that then the house was filled with a cloud, even the house of the LORD; (14) So that the priests could not stand to minister by reason of the cloud: for the glory of the LORD had filled the house of God.*

***Revelation 15:8** And the temple was filled with smoke from the glory of God and from His power; and no one could enter the temple until the seven plagues of the seven angels were completed.*

***Exodus 40:35** Moses was not able to enter the tent of meeting because the cloud had settled on it, and the glory of the LORD filled the tabernacle.*

***1 Chronicles 16:34** O give thanks to the LORD, for He is good; For His lovingkindness is everlasting.*

Friends, many gospel singers, musicians, and ministers have failed God, but you can be God's True Worshipper.

CHAPTER THREE

THE REALMS OF PRAISE AND WORSHIP

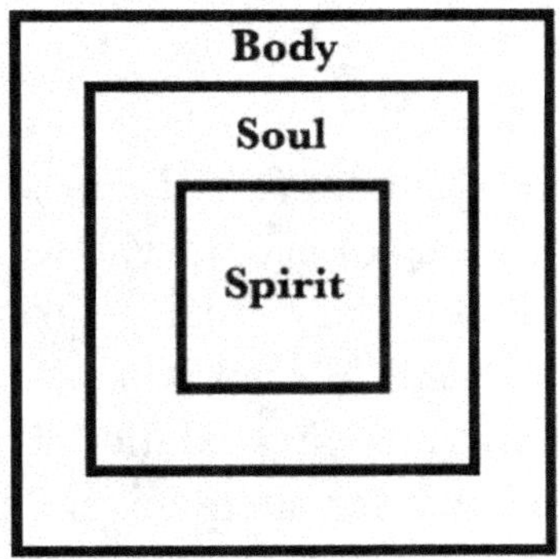

There are three realms of praise and worship: The Outer Court, the Holy Place, and the Holy of Holies. True Praise and worship begins in the Outer Court, moves into the Holy Place and ends in the Holy of Holies where communion takes place between Divinity and humanity.

Just as the old sanctuary was built in three divisions, likewise, the Lord God divided our bodies into three parts, (the Spirit, Soul, and Body). Our worship must also go through these three stages. Some people are comfortable with remaining in the first stage (the Outer Court), others make it to the second stage (the Holy Place), but it takes true worshippers to reach the third stage (the Holy of Holies).

Outer Court worshippers worship in the flesh. The Holy Place worshippers worship in the soul realm, or the place of desire (intellect, will, and emotion). Both end up not reaching the Holy of Holies (the place of communion with God) due to their lack of preparation, lack of seriousness, unholy living and other sinful behaviors (the deeds of the flesh, or, the old self, the sinful nature of man). But those that do prepare and are committed to doing all that is required of them by the Lord can reach the Holy of Holies through the blood of Jesus. This is why the Lord is calling for true worshippers who will worship in Spirit and in Truth.

Outer Court Worshippers (The Flesh or Bodily Realm)
This refers to the group of people who worship God but are in the flesh or bodily realm. Their worship remains in the Outer Court as a result of inadequate preparation towards their worship, failure to live a life of discipline, pride, lateness to church, divided attention, etc. In this case, these worshippers limit themselves to little or no experience with God. Their worship remains in the bodily stage, and they aren't able to experience effective communion with God which exists in the next stages ahead.

Heb 9:1-10 (NET) *"1Now the first covenant, in fact, had regulations for worship and its earthly sanctuary. 2 For a tent was prepared, the outer one, which contained the lampstand, the table, and the presentation of the loaves; this is called the holy place. 3 And after the second curtain there was a tent called the Holy of Holies. 4 It contained the golden altar of incense and the ark of the covenant covered entirely with gold. In this ark were the golden urn containing the manna, Aaron's rod that budded, and the stone tablets of the covenant. 5 And above the ark were the cherubim of glory overshadowing the mercy seat. Now is not the time to speak of these things in detail. 6 So with these things prepared like this, the priests enter continually into the outer tent as they perform their duties. 7 But only the high priest enters once a year into the inner tent, and not without blood that he offers for himself and for the sins of the people committed in ignorance. 8 The Holy Spirit is making clear that the way into the holy place had not yet appeared as long as the old tabernacle was standing. 9 This was a symbol for the time then present, when gifts and sacrifices were offered that could not perfect the conscience of the worshiper. 10 They served only for matters of food and drink and various washings; they are external regulations imposed until the new order came."*

Inner Court/Holy Place Worshippers (The realm of Desire or the Soul Realm)

With a higher level of commitment, preparation and seriousness, some people can move from their fleshly stage of worship to a soul- or desiring-realm as it is written in Psalm 42. The Holy Place is an awesome place where you yearn to know more about the Lord. Those who reach this stage, the soul realm, must press hard, continuously, to be able to reach the next stage.

***Psalm 42:1-5** <<To the chief Musician, Maschil, for the sons of Korah. >> As the hart panteth after the water brooks, so panteth my soul after thee, O God. {Maschil...: or, A Psalm giving instruction of the sons, etc} {panteth: Heb. brayeth} 2 My soul thirsteth for God, for the living God: when shall I come and appear before God? 3 My tears have been my meat day and night, while they continually say unto me, Where is thy God? 4 When I remember these things, I pour out my soul in me: for I had gone with the* *multitude, I went with them to the house of God, with the voice of joy and praise, with a multitude that kept holyday. 5 Why art thou cast down, O my soul? and why art thou disquieted in me? hope thou in God: for I shall yet praise him for the help of his countenance. {cast: Heb. bowed} {praise: or, give thanks} {for the...: or, his presence is salvation}*

Holy of Holies (A Realm of Fellowship or Place of Communion)

Those who can reach the Holy of Holies in their worship are people who are sincerely committed to the things of God and are prepared in their hearts with all seriousness to live their lives to please the Lord. Such people can move from the fleshly stage of worship to the soul-realm, and, ultimately, reach the spiritual realm or the Holy of Holies where they have communion with the Lord and remain in His presence.

***Psalm 91:1-16(KJV)**. "He that dwelleth in the secret place of the most High shall abide under the shadow of the Almighty. {Abide: Heb. lodge} 2 I will say of the LORD, He is my refuge and my fortress: my God; in him will I trust. 3 Surely he shall deliver thee from the snare of the fowler, and from the noisome pestilence. 4 He shall cover thee with his feathers, and under his wings shalt thou trust: his truth shall be thy shield and buckler. 5 Thou shalt not be afraid for the terror by night; nor for the arrow that flieth by day; 6 Nor for the pestilence that walketh in darkness; nor for the destruction that wasteth at noonday. 7 A thousand shall fall at thy side, and ten thousand at thy right hand; but it shall not come nigh thee. 8 Only with thine eyes shalt thou behold and see* *the reward of the wicked.9 Because thou hast made the LORD, which is my refuge, even the most High, thy habitation; 10 There shall no evil befall thee, neither shall any plague come nigh thy dwelling. 11 For he shall give his angels charge over thee, to keep thee in all thy ways. 12 They shall bear thee up in their hands, lest thou dash thy foot against a stone. 13 Thou shalt tread upon the lion and adder: the young lion and the dragon shalt thou trample under feet. {adder: or, asp} 14 Because he hath set his love upon me, therefore will I deliver him: I will set him on high, because he hath known my name. 15 He shall call upon me, and I will answer him: I will be with him in trouble; I will deliver him, and honour him. 16 With long life will I satisfy him, and shew him my salvation. {long...: Heb. length of days}".*

In this realm of worship, "Deep calls for deep" and everything is possible, except sin.

Psalm 42:7-8(KJV) *Deep calleth unto deep at the noise of thy waterspouts: all thy waves and thy billows are gone over me. 8Yet the LORD will command his lovingkindness in the daytime, and in the night his song shall be with me, and my prayer unto the God of my life"*

The realm you can reach is determined by how willing and obedient you are to fellowship with the Holy Spirit; for He is always ready to give without measure.

John3.34 *"For he whom God hath sent speaketh the words of God: for God giveth not the Spirit by measure unto him."*

The reason why many people are not able to enter into God's gates and into His holy presence is that most Christians in this generation desire to worship God on their own terms and not according to the divine order set for us by the Lord. In Psalm 100, David described the character of the one who is to give praise and worship to God. He states that such a person must do so gladly and joyfully. The approach to God's gates and His presence is through thanksgiving or the giving of praises.

> ***Psalm 100.1-5(KJV)*** *" <<A Psalm of praise. >> Make a joyful noise unto the LORD, all ye lands. {praise: or, thanksgiving} {all...: Heb. all the earth} 2 Serve the LORD with gladness: come before his presence with singing. 3 Know ye that the LORD he is God: it is he that hath made us, and not we ourselves; we are his people, and the sheep of his pasture. {and not...: or, and his we are} 4 Enter into his gates with thanksgiving, and into his courts with praise: be thankful unto him, and bless his name. 5 For the LORD is good; his mercy is everlasting; and his truth endureth to all generations. (to all...: Heb. to generation and generation)."*

We can only enter into God's presence, the Holy of Holies, through the blood of Jesus

God told Moses to warn the Priests of old to never come before Him without blood. The blood is symbolic of a covenant and the purging of sins. We can see, in the New Testament, that the same thing is required of us today. Without the blood of Jesus, it is impossible to enter into the Holy of Holies, into His presence. This is the very reason why the church must be knowledgeable about the blood of the Lamb of God (the covenant with Jesus). We must treat the blood of Jesus (our covenant with Him) with all respect and with honor, knowing that none of us are qualified to enter into His presence without the blood. Without the blood, our sins remain. We must reverence the blood covenant and apply the blood to gain access to the Holy of Holies to have communion with God through our worship.

Hebrews 10.18-29(KJV) " *Now where remission of these is, there is no more offering for sin.* **19 Having therefore, brethren, boldness to enter into the holies by the blood of Jesus, {boldness: or, liberty}** *20 By a new and living way, which he hath consecrated for us, through the veil, that is to say, his flesh; {consecrated: or, new made} 21 And having an high priest over the house of God; 22 Let us draw near with a true heart in full assurance of faith, having our hearts sprinkled from an evil conscience, and our bodies washed with pure water. 23 Let us hold fast the profession of our faith without wavering; (for he is faithful that promised;) 24And let us consider one another to provoke unto love and to good works: 25Not forsaking the assembling of ourselves together, as the manner of some is; but exhorting one another: and so much the more, as ye see the day approaching. 26For if we sin wilfully after that we have received the knowledge of the truth, there remaineth no more sacrifice for sins, 27But a certain fearful looking for of judgment and fiery indignation, which shall devour the adversaries. 28He that despised Moses' law died without mercy under two or three witnesses: 29Of how much sorer* *punishment, suppose ye, shall he be thought worthy, who hath trodden under foot the Son of God, and hath counted the blood of the covenant, wherewith he was sanctified, an unholy thing, and hath done despite unto the Spirit of grace?"*

Hebrews9:1-14 (KJV) *"Then verily the first covenant had also ordinances of divine service, and a worldly sanctuary. {ordinances: or, ceremonies} 2 For there was a tabernacle made; the first, wherein was the candlestick, and the table, and the shewbread; which is called the sanctuary. {the sanctuary: or, holy} 3And after the second veil, the tabernacle which is called the Holies of all; 4Which had the golden censer, and the ark of the covenant overlaid round about with gold, wherein was the golden pot that had manna, and Aaron's rod that budded, and the tables of the covenant; 5And over it the cherubims of glory shadowing the mercyseat; of which we cannot now speak particularly. 6Now when these things were thus ordained, the priests went always into the first tabernacle, accomplishing the service of God. 7But into the second went the high priest alone once every year, not without blood, which he offered for himself, and for the errors of the people: 8The Holy Ghost this signifying, that the way into the holies of all was not yet made manifest, while as the first tabernacle was yet standing: 9Which was a figure for the time then present, in which were offered both gifts and sacrifices, that could not make him that did the service perfect, as pertaining to the conscience; 10Which stood only in meats and drinks,* *and divers washings, and carnal ordinances, imposed on them until the time of reformation. {ordinances: or, rites, or, ceremonies} 11But Christ being come an high priest of good things to come, by a greater and more perfect tabernacle, not made with hands, that is to say, not of this building; 12Neither by the blood of goats and calves, but by his own blood he entered in once into the holy place, having obtained eternal redemption for us. 13For if the blood of bulls and of goats, and the ashes of an heifer sprinkling the unclean, sanctifieth to the purifying of the flesh: 14How much more shall the blood of Christ, who through the eternal Spirit offered himself without spot to God, purge your conscience from dead works to serve the living God? {spot: or, fault}.*

Note: Hebrews chapter 7, 8, 9, and 10.

It is ordained that we must begin our worship in Outer Court, because, although we are spiritual beings, we have souls and dwell in bodies of flesh. We must understand, however, that we cannot allow our worship to remain in the Outer Court or in the realm of the flesh. Rather, we must always be willing and prepared to enter through the blood of Jesus and to move past the Holy Place and into the Holy of Holies. Just as there are three realms or stages of prayer, there are also three levels or realms of praise and worship; and for us to touch God's heart, we must move from the Outer Court (the flesh), through the Inner Court (the soul-realm), and then enter finally into the spiritual realm (His Presence), where communion with God truly takes place. God is spirit and those who worship Him must worship Him in spirit and in truth. You must be in the spirit to enter and remain in God's presence.

The Three Realms

The Bodily Realm – the first stage; the flesh.
The Soul Realm – the second stage; the place to surrender and to deaden one's evil desires, will, intellect, emotions, etc.
The Spiritual Realm – the third stage; the stage where we enter into His presence.

Our revelation of who God is in our lives causes us to worship Him

> *Ps 63:1-2a Psalm of David, when he was in the wilderness of Judah. O God, thou art my God; early will I seek thee: my soul thirsteth for thee, my flesh longeth for thee in a dry and thirsty land, where no water is; {thirsty: Heb. weary} {where...: without water} 2 To see thy power and thy glory, so as I have seen thee in the sanctuary.*

The pattern of our worship: spirit and truth

> *John 4:24 God is a Spirit: and they that worship him must worship him in spirit and in truth.*

Our approach to God in worship:
- With a true heart
- In faith
- With a conscience purified by the blood of Jesus
- In the Word of God
- In unity and agreement with the saints of God

\-   In agreement with the Lord

Hebrews 10:22 Let us draw near with a true heart in full assurance of faith, having our hearts sprinkled from an evil conscience, and our bodies washed with pure water

Matthew 18:19-20 Again I say unto you, That if two of you shall agree on earth as touching anything that they shall ask, it shall be done for them of my Father which is in heaven. 20 For where two or three are gathered together in my name, there am I in the midst of them.

Types of godly worship
- ❖ Prayer-Worship or Worship as a form of prayer
- ❖ Reverence-Worship
- ❖ Live-Worship
- ❖ Song-based Worship

There are different types of worship patterns that churches, and individuals present to God based on their culture, location, ministry, etc. As long as their intent is good and it is in line with the word of God, God is pleased with and receives their worship. To present the kind of worship that is sweet and acceptable to the Lord, and one that can move the Lord to act in our midst, the worshipper must understand how to operate in the grace and the ministry that God has given to them. For example, if you have the ministry of healing and deliverance, you must know how to create an atmosphere that proclaims the nature of the Lord as a healer and deliverer, that He may be pleased enough to move and meet the needs of His people. This example is prayer-worship. In that kind of worship, the worshipper does not make requests of the Lord, as that would then be defined as a different form of prayer, and no longer prayer-worship. The prayer suddenly becomes worship, prayer-worship to be specific. Since, in it, the worshipper magnifies the nature of the Lord.

Worshippers must take note of the following:

1. **Having good intentions and the right motive**
   Every acceptable worship must be backed by good intentions and right motives. Remember that He, the Lord, judges the motives and intent of the heart before He accepts anything that is presented to Him.

2. **Preparation**
   Consider the fact that it is before the Lord God Almighty's presence that you are going. Therefore, never present anything unholy or unpleasant like Cain's offering. Your song preparation, selection, arrangement, training, instrumentation, rehearsals, and worship as a whole must be done properly. Above all, you must prepare yourself by living a holy life for Him, because He is holy.

3. **Presentation**
   Here, the ministers or instrumentalists present everything they have arranged. They must be sensitive and must make sure that the way they present their musical arrangement meets the requirements of the occasion. They must also make sure to present everything boldly, confidently, and powerfully. To bring good results, you must make sure to do your part to work on your presentation during the rehearsal time before the actual service.

Prayer Worship (Worship as a form of prayer)

Prayer worship is an act of expressing our reverence unto God by combining the scriptures, songs of worship, and exaltation, with prayer. It is the act of proclaiming the greatness of God and placing Him on the highest pedestal. True prayer-worship brings results. This form of worship goes beyond thanksgiving. It is where you tell God who He is; where you proclaim His greatness, His power, His authority, His might and all of His attributes. Unlike in reverence worship where the worshipper goes before the Lord in brokenness and with a contrite heart, in prayer worship, the worshipper uses the revelation of the word and songs along with proclamations about the nature of God, to declare His majesty powerfully. This form of worship and prayer easily unfolds the hands of God and is also able to break satanic barriers as we declare His attributes.

Scriptures: The scriptures you chose in your presentation and exaltation must support one another and the attribute of God that you are emphasizing in your worship.

Song Selection: Remember that the songs selected for the prayer-worship must also be in agreement with your words of exaltation, scriptures, and prayer in order to bring out a revelation so that the congregation can also worship based on the revelation of the word, songs, and scripture to declare His attributes.

> *Acts 16:16-19 "And it came to pass as we went to prayer a certain damsel possessed with a spirit of divination met us, which brought her masters much gain by soothsaying. The same followed Paul and us,*

and cried saying, these men are the servant of the most High God, which shows unto us the way of salvation. And this did She many days But Paul, being grieved turned and said to the spirit, I command thee in the name of Jesus to come out of her, and he came out the same hour. And when her master saw that the hope of their gains was gone, they caught Paul and Silas and drew them unto the marketplace unto the rulers".

Note VS. 23-28

23After they had been severely flogged, they were thrown into prison, and the jailer was commanded to guard them carefully. 24Upon receiving such orders, he put them in the inner cell and fastened their feet in the stocks. 25About midnight Paul and Silas were praying and singing hymns to God, and the other prisoners were listening to them. 26Suddenly there was such a violent earthquake that the foundations of the prison were shaken. At once all the prison doors flew open, and everybody's chains came loose. 27The jailer woke up, and when he saw the prison doors open, he drew his sword and was about to kill himself because he thought the prisoners had escaped. 28But Paul shouted, "Don't harm yourself! We are all here!"

Even in times of trouble, whether you have been whipped, beaten, put in prison or in chains, etc., do not be downcast but declare the glory of God by praying and singing hymns.

Furthermore, prayer-worship is where you combine spiritual songs, hymns, instrumentations (music), and scriptures to tell the Lord God who He is and to proclaim His attributes, abilities, and works. When it is done well, faithfully, and powerfully, prayer-worship carries the power and anointing that is able to break down demonic walls, barriers, and many more. So, in the deepest valleys of your life, do not cry, but rather lift up your eyes in prayer-worship and you will see the performance of the Lord like the Apostle Paul and Silas. However, for prayer-worship to be done well, you must have an understanding of prayer, have scriptures for exaltation, and know how to connect those scriptures with the songs and instrumentation to give a proper presentation that yields results. When the Lord accepts the sweet-smelling fragrance of your offering, His spirit will take control over the worship, the environment, and the entire atmosphere and His glory, which is His presence, will fill the place, causing a release of anointing, power, and unction, making everything possible.

What is Prayer?

Prayer is simply our way of communicating with the Lord. So what I call "Prayer Worship" (worship as a form of prayer) is where you communicate with the Lord, but in a way that honors and reveres His greatness.

When God created the heavens and the earth, He ordained Adam as the governor of this earth. In doing this, God gave him the authority to rule and to reign. Therefore, He doesn't just interfere with worldly affairs. This is why He instituted prayer, to allow us to give Him the authority to intervene in human affairs. Prayer, therefore, can be defined as an earthly license that allows heaven to operate on the earth. Prayer is our petition, supplication or communion with God. Jesus taught that men ought to pray (Luke 18:1). We are urged to seek the Lord (Isaiah 55:6), to ask and seek (Matthew 7:7), to watch (Matthew 26: 41) and to pray (Luke 22:41), to pray always (Ephesians 6:18), to be careful for nothing (Phi 4:6), to pray without ceasing (1 Thessalonians 5:17) and to pray with thanksgiving (Colossians 4:2).

There are many kinds of prayer. For example, there is warfare prayer, supplication, thanksgiving, the prayer of request, etc. So, what makes prayer-worship different than the other kinds of prayer? In prayer-worship, the worshipper does not make requests of the Lord, as that would then be defined as the prayer of supplication or request, warfare, etc., and no longer prayer-worship. Rather, the worshipper declares the nature and attributes of the Lord, as it is found in the scripture, in combination with songs and exaltation, in a musically skillful way to offer the Lord the sweet-smelling worship that pleases Him to move in the capacity of the attribute you are declaring. It pleases the Lord to manifest Himself as you proclaim His nature. The prayer, presented to the Lord in this manner, suddenly becomes worship, prayer-worship to be specific. Since, in it, the worshipper magnifies the nature of the Lord.

In conclusion, prayer-worship gives us, the people of God, the opportunity to go before the throne of grace to proclaim His majestic attributes in a powerful way. Psalm 145

Reverence-worship

Reverence worship is the act of reverencing the Lord our God with the sounds of continuous strings, the grand piano, the harp, and trumpets. Reverence worship is unlike prayer-worship where the worshippers are very active. When reverence-worship is accepted by God, He responds by demonstrating His power in the midst of the congregation. Reverence worship is the kind of worship that causes the worshippers to be still before the Lord (Psalm 46.10-11). In this kind of worship, the worship leaders or music ministry is more easily able to lead the congregation to a point of brokenness before the Lord to proclaim His nature. It is such humility that opens the door or allows the Lord to move amongst the congregation.

Psalm 51.15-17 (KJV) O Lord, open thou my lips; and my mouth shall shew forth thy praise. 16For thou desirest not sacrifice; else would I give it: thou delightest not in burnt offering. {else...: or, that I should} 17The sacrifices of God are a broken spirit: a broken and a contrite heart, O God, thou wilt not despise.

Psalm34.18(KJV)"The LORD is nigh unto them that are of a broken heart; and saveth such as be of a contrite spirit. {unto...: Heb. to the broken of heart} {of a contrite...: Heb. contrite of spirit}".

Isaiah57(KJV) "For thus saith the high and lofty One that inhabiteth eternity, whose name is Holy; I dwell in the high and holy place, with him also that is of a contrite and humble spirit, to revive the spirit of the humble, and to revive the heart of the contrite ones.";

Isaiah 66.2 For all those things hath mine handmade, and all those things have been, saith the LORD: but to this man will I look, even to him that is poor and of a contrite spirit, and trembleth at my word."

Furthermore, reverence-worship is where we express our appreciation and reverence to God in a humble manner. In this kind of worship, the worshipper proclaims the greatness of God, placing Him on the highest pedestal through the brokenness of heart. This brings powerful results even as we honor the King of kings and the Lord of lords.

Live Worship

Live worship is a unique type of worship. While it can share many similarities with other forms of worship, such as the prayer, reverence, and song-based worship types, live worship is unique in the way in which it involves more interaction with and the involvement of the audience, congregation, or listeners. Live worship can occur in various settings such as the church, a studio, radio station, or even in a gospel event or program. Like the other forms of worship, the aim of live worship is to honor the Lord Jesus Christ, the Master Owner, for His Lordship. Although live worship is still an act of reverencing the Lord, there is a need to keep the audience alive, active, excited, and motivated, so that those who have come together would not feel bored, uninterested, tired, drained, etc. Because of the increased communication with the audience, ministers often perform this kind of worship in a live gospel event or program.

Song-based Worship

What I call the "Song-based worship" is the type of worship where a series of nice worship songs are put together and beautifully sung in the honor of our Lord and King. This kind of worship places more emphasis on using the songs to minister to the people. There are a lot of churches that practice this type of worship. In their worship sessions, they worship through their songs alone. Those who excel in this kind of worship are able to use their vocal talent or instrumentation to lay emphasis on or draw special attention to certain words of the song, note, or chord to declare the attributes of God.

Praises

Praise is an act of expressing joy, excitement, gratitude, thanksgiving, and appreciation to the Lord. Praise often involves expressions like singing, dancing, clapping, the lifting of hands, making of joyful noises, etc. It is the act or moment of rejoicing in the Lord with a lifted spirit, soul, and body. Praise excites you before the Lord. The Lord inhabits in the praise of His people, so the purpose of praise is to chair Him in the midst of the congregation.

Kinds of praise

Location, denomination, culture, and environment play a major role in the kind of praise that must be sung. For example, almost all Africans play upbeat rhythms, especially fast and mid-tempo beats and rhythms, both francophones and anglophones, in their times of praise. Meanwhile, praise songs in locations like the United States, Europe, Asia, and

Australia, tend to have more variation in tempos and rhythms depending on the types of songs. A common quality that we see in praise songs across all the continents is that the songs are always moving and fit for dancing, clapping, etc. unlike worship, that often causes one to be broken in humility before the Lord with actions such as kneeling, crying and weeping, before the Lord.

Praise songs can be categorized in the following ways:

❖ **Fast praise:**
This is the kind of praise where the tempo of both the songs and the instruments are very fast. Here, all the actions such as dancing, clapping, lifting of hands, etc., are done at a very fast pace.

❖ **Mid-tempo praise:**
This is the kind of praise where the tempo for both the songs and the instruments are in a mid-tempo. This kind of praise is neither fast nor slow.

❖ **Worship-tempo praise:**
What I call "worship-tempo praise" is the kind of praise where the tempo is not fast enough to be considered to be mid-tempo.

Special Song Ministrations

Special song ministrations can be performed as a solo, duet, or even as a group. The ministrations may be worship or praise, etc. They are performed to inspire and encourage the listeners. In special song ministrations, the ministers perform to glorify God and God also uses their ministration to uplift, to warn, to edify, and to send various forms of messages to His people.

Ephesians 5:19 NKJV speaking to one another in psalms and hymns and spiritual songs, singing and making melody in your heart to the Lord,

1 Corinthians 14:26 BSB What then shall we say, brothers? When you come together, everyone has a hymn or a teaching, a revelation, a tongue, or an interpretation. All of these must be done to build up the church.

Colossians 3:16 NKJV Let the word of Christ dwell in you richly in all wisdom, teaching and admonishing one another in psalms and hymns and spiritual songs, singing with grace in your hearts to the Lord.

Psalm 95:2 BSB Let us enter His presence with thanksgiving; let us make a joyful noise to Him in song.

Preparation before true praise and worship is offered

Whenever the preparation meets the requirements of the Lord, there are always great results. This is the very reason why the Lord always prepares the people He wants to use before using them. The truth is that the Lord desires to prepare us, but we must be willing to open up for that preparation. We must accept the Lord's preparation or else we will not be equipped to do whatever He has called us to do. We see from the beginning of creation that God prepares everyone He uses. God prepared Adam, the first man, by giving him instructions before assigning him the task of ruling, managing, and nurturing the Garden of Eden. He prepared Abraham to use him by entering into a covenant with him and by setting him apart from the gods of his parent's house and country in order to prepare him for the promise. Likewise, He prepared Israel, the Judges, and the prophets. He also prepared Moses and used Moses to prepare Joshua and Eliezer the Priest. He used Elijah to prepare Elisha. Jesus prepared the Apostles and used the Apostles to prepare the early church. God is still in the business of preparing to use any willing vessel who desires to study to show themselves approved. Even our Lord Jesus Christ was prepared, tested in the wilderness, and approved before starting His public ministry.

Areas where true worshippers need preparation

1. Preparation of the heart

As a worshipper, the intent of your heart must be right. If your heart isn't right with God, your worship wouldn't be acceptable. You must be free and not troubled. May the Lord fully establish His throne in your heart. You must learn to surrender your heart fully unto Him.

2. Preparation of the mind

As a worshipper, fixing your mind on heavenly things is very important because your motives must be right and acceptable before Him. The aim of your praise and worship shouldn't be for selfish gain and vain glory. Free your mind from worldly matters and refuse to allow Satan to use your mind as a battlefield. Fill your mind with scriptures about God and who He is. Prepare your mind for worship by meditating on the word of God.

3. Preparation of the body

Present your body as a living sacrifice; holy and acceptable unto the Lord. Be willing to give your body unto Him; that is, to lead a consecrated and holy life.

4. Preparation of the soul

Surrender your soul by giving up your will, emotion, and intellect. Desire the Lord more, exalt, encourage, and allow your soul to enjoy God's presence. Remember that it is best to lift your soul with God's word if your soul is downcast.

5. Preparation of the spirit

Allow your spirit to bear witness with the Holy Spirit. Fellowship and have communion with Him. Let deep call for deep. Worship Him with your spirit in Spirit and in Truth.

6. Musical Preparation

Select songs, arrange them and attend rehearsals to learn the songs. Master the parts, notes, chords progression and musical arrangements with the instrumentalists. Work on balancing the sounds and the vocals. Dedicate enough time on presentation. Conclude on which type of presentation to create before the service.

7. Preparation by the Word

Allow the word of God to prepare you; read, study, memorize and meditate on it. Practice how to present the word in connection with song selections and arrangements.

8. Preparation through prayers

Wait before the Lord to receive songs for the ministration. When you receive them, ask for directions concerning the arrangements and presentation. Commit the worship leaders and the entire worship team, including the instrumentalists, into God's hands to grant them enough oil/anointing to perform. Commit the congregation before the Lord to give them a heart of worship and praise. Pray against everything including evil spirits and sins that will hinder and interfere with your praise and worship. Ask the Lord to command angels of praise and worship to come and minister with you. Ask the Lord to sit enthroned in your praise and worship and ask Him to receive your worship and praise and to work through the ministration for His presence and glory to be seen.

9. Preparation of the Congregation or Assembly

Every Godly institution needs to know that there is a need for preparation before meeting with the Lord. The people of God must be educated and trained to prepare themselves before appearing before the Lord. This will help the congregation to become mature concerning the need for setting themselves apart and it will encourage them to make every effort to keep themselves holy and ready to meet with the Lord.

Ezra 7.9 -10(KJV) For upon the first day of the first month began he to go up from Babylon, and on the first day of the fifth month came he to Jerusalem, according to the good hand of his God upon him. {began...: Heb. was the foundation of the going up} 10 For Ezra had prepared his heart to seek the law of the LORD, and to do it, and to teach in Israel statutes and judgments.

Proverbs 22.6(KJV) Train up a child in the way he should go: and when he is old, he will not depart from it. {Train...: or, Catechise} {in...: Heb. in his way}

2Timothy2.14-26(KJV) *"Of these things put them in remembrance, charging them before the Lord that they strive not about words to no profit, but to the subverting of the hearers. 15 Study to shew thyself approved unto God, a workman that needeth not to be ashamed, rightly dividing the word of truth. 16 But shun profane and vain babblings: for they will increase unto more ungodliness. 17 And their word will eat as doth a canker: of whom is Hymenaeus and Philetus; {canker: or, gangrene} 18 Who concerning the truth have erred, saying that the resurrection is past already; and overthrow the faith of some. 19 Nevertheless the foundation of God standeth sure, having this seal, The Lord knoweth them that are his. And, Let every one that nameth the name of Christ depart from iniquity. {sure: or, steady} 20 But in a great house there are not only vessels of gold and of silver, but also of wood and of earth; and some to honour, and some to dishonour. 21 If a man therefore purge himself from these, he shall be a vessel unto honour, sanctified, and meet for the master's use, and prepared unto every good work. 22 Flee also youthful lusts: but follow righteousness, faith, charity, peace, with them that call on the Lord out of a pure heart. 23 But foolish and unlearned questions avoid, knowing that they do gender strifes. 24 And the servant of the Lord must not strive; but be gentle unto all men, apt to teach, patient, {patient: or, forbearing} 25 In meekness instructing those that oppose themselves; if God peradventure will give them repentance to the acknowledging of the truth; 26 And that they may recover themselves out of the snare of the devil, who are taken captive by him at his will. {recover...: Gr. awake} {taken...: Gr. taken alive}*

__2 Timothty4.1-5(KJV)__ charge thee therefore before God, and the Lord Jesus Christ, who shall judge the quick and the dead at his appearing and his kingdom; 2 Preach the word; be instant in season, out of season; reprove, rebuke, exhort with all longsuffering and doctrine. 3 For the time will come when they will not endure sound doctrine; but after their own lusts shall they heap to themselves teachers, having itching ears; 4 And they shall turn away their ears from the truth, and shall be turned unto fables. 5 But watch thou in all things, endure afflictions, do the work of an evangelist, make full proof of thy ministry. {make...; or, fulfil}

__2Timothy1:1-14.__ according to the promise of life which is in Christ Jesus, 2 To Timothy, my dearly beloved son: Grace, mercy, and peace, from God the Father and Christ Jesus our Lord. 3 I thank God, whom I serve from my forefathers with pure conscience, that without ceasing I have remembrance of thee in my prayers night and day; 4 Greatly desiring to see thee, being mindful of thy tears, that I may be filled with joy; {Greatly...: or, remembering thy tears, I greatly desire to see thee that} 5 When I call to remembrance the unfeigned faith that is in thee, which dwelt first in thy grandmother Lois, and thy mother Eunice; and I am persuaded that in thee also. 6 Wherefore I put thee in remembrance that thou stir up the gift of God, which is in thee by the putting on of my hands. 7 For God hath not given us the spirit of fear; but of power, and of love, and of a sound mind. 8 Be not thou therefore ashamed of the testimony of our Lord, nor of me his prisoner: but be thou partaker of the afflictions of the gospel according to the power of God; 9 Who hath saved us, and called us with an holy calling, not according to our works, but according to his own purpose and grace, which was given us in Christ

Jesus before the world began, 10 But is now made manifest by the appearing of our Saviour Jesus Christ, who hath abolished death, and hath brought life and immortality to light through the gospel: 11 Whereunto I am appointed a preacher, and an apostle, and a teacher of the Gentiles. 12 For the which cause I also suffer these things: nevertheless I am not ashamed: for I know whom I have believed, and am persuaded that he is able to keep that which I have committed unto him against that day. {believed: or, trusted} 13 Hold fast the form of sound words, which thou hast heard of me, in faith and love which is in Christ Jesus. 14That good thing which was committed unto thee keep by the Holy Ghost which dwelleth in us.

In conclusion, preparation is needed in every area of life and in God's work; and, without it, none can fulfill their prophetic destiny.

An excerpt from "Fresh Manna", by Bishop Dr. Emmanuel D. Apau Jr.

WHEN PREPARATION MEETS DIVINE REQUIREMENTS:

Success or failure in the things of God, and even in the secular world depends on how one prepares himself/herself to meet the set standards.

To fulfill your destiny in this life, according to God's perfect will and even to make it to Heaven (Eternity) depends on how seriously you take these very powerful keys:

a) Preparation, dedication, devotion, and determination of heart;

b) The willingness to seek the Lord and study;

c) Observation, obedience, the practice of what you have learned or what you preach

d) Teaching, impartation, the raising of disciples or followers;

e) Presentation, the correct way to deliver your message and present your worship in order to impact both heaven and the lives of those in the congregation is very important to God and it can be done properly through good preparation.

Ezra 7:10For Ezra had prepared his heart to seek the law of the LORD, and to do it, and to teach in Israel statutes and judgments. Proverbs 16.1The preparations of the heart belong to man, But the answer of the tongue is from the Lord. Ezra 7:11This is a copy of the letter King Artaxerxes had given to Ezra the priest, a teacher of the Law, a man learned in matters concerning the commands and decrees of the LORD for Israel: Deuteronomy 33:10He teaches your precepts to Jacob and your law to Israel. He offers incense before you and whole burnt offerings on your altar.

Are you a prepared vessel for the Lord?

CHAPTER FOUR

PRAISE AND WORSHIP IS DIVINELY ORDAINED

Praise and worship is divinely ordained. God established them to be part and parcel of His kingdom and they cannot be taken away. Again, praise and worship will never pass. Humans, as well the entire heavenly host, were created to practice praise and worship. The angels are still doing it right now and the powerful thing about it is that, in the kingdom to come, praise and worship will continue. All the redeemed will be part of it, joining together with the heavenly choir (ministering spirits) to sing even better songs to glorify our Lord and King forever and ever.

Revelation 4:6-11 (KJV) "And before the throne there was a sea of glass like unto crystal: and in the midst of the throne, and round about the throne, were four beasts full of eyes before and behind. 7 And the first beast was like a lion, and the second beast like a calf, and the third beast had a face as a man, and the fourth beast was like a flying eagle.8 And the four beasts had each of them six wings about him; and they were full of eyes within: and they rest not day and night, saying, Holy, holy, holy, Lord God Almighty, which was, and is, and is to come. {rest...: Gr. have no rest} 9 And when those beasts give glory and honour and thanks to him that sat on the throne, who liveth for ever and ever, 10 The four and twenty elders fall down before him that sat on the throne, and worship him that liveth for ever and ever, and cast their crowns before the throne, saying, 11 Thou art worthy, O Lord, to receive glory and honour and power: for thou hast created all things, and for thy pleasure they are and were created".

Revelation 5:6-14 (KJV) *"And I beheld, and, lo, in the midst of the throne and of the four beasts, and in the midst of the elders, stood a Lamb as it had been slain, having seven horns and seven eyes, which are the seven Spirits of God sent forth into all the earth. 7 And he came and took the book out of the right hand of him that sat upon the throne. 8 And when he had taken the book, the four beasts and four and twenty elders fell down before the Lamb, having every one of them harps, and golden vials full of odours, which are the prayers of saints. {odours: or, incense} 9 And they sung a new song, saying, Thou art worthy to take the book, and to open the seals thereof: for thou wast slain, and hast redeemed us to God by thy blood out of every kindred, and tongue, and people, and nation; 10 And hast made us unto our God kings and priests: and we shall reign on the earth. 11 And I beheld, and I heard the voice of many angels round about the throne and the beasts and the elders: and the number of them was ten thousand times ten thousand, and thousands of thousands; 12 Saying with a loud voice, Worthy is the Lamb that was slain to receive power, and riches, and wisdom, and strength, and honour, and glory, and blessing. 13 And every creature which is in heaven, and on the earth, and under the earth, and such as are in the sea, and all that are in them, heard I saying, Blessing, and honour, and glory, and power, be unto him that sitteth upon the throne, and unto the Lamb for ever and ever. 14 And*

Folks, everything that has breath must worship and praise God, for all were made to worship Him. Most of all, we must remember that a special day is coming, and it is coming quickly, when the redeemed will sing a song which the heavenly host (the Angels) will not be able to understand. Friends, let us live to worship God now, for a better moment of unceasing worship is drawing near in the coming city, the New Jerusalem.

Revelation 4:2-4 (KJV) And I heard a sound from heaven like the roar of mighty ocean waves or the rolling of loud thunder. It was like the sound of many harpists playing together. This great choir sang a wonderful new song in front of the throne of God and before the four living beings and the twenty-four elders. No one could learn this song except the 144,000 who had been redeemed from the earth. They have kept themselves as pure as virgins, following the Lamb wherever he goes. They have been purchased from among the people on the earth as a special offering to God and to the Lamb.

CHAPTER FIVE

LIVE PRAISE AND WORSHIP EVENT/PROGRAM

A live praise and worship event or program is a kind of service where worship songs, song ministrations, solos, and praises are combined with special instrumentation to perform in a live setting in order to give the Lord the highest praise and worship. Note that in a live gospel event, various kinds of songs are acceptable because it is a special event. This kind of special program involves preparing and putting different worshippers, gospel singers, musicians, people of all ages, godly talent, and race together with a genuine aim to worship and praise Yahweh, the Lord Jesus Christ, to give Him the highest honor. It is the type of service where the worshippers and the musicians perform live to honor Jesus Christ, the King of the kings, Yahweh, the Master Owner of all things, for His Lordship.

In the live program, you can put different types of gospel artists together that can edify the congregation and also accomplish the main goal of glorifying the Lord. In this kind of event, different gospel ministers are invited to come together to perform live from different angles and with various styles. Since it is a live performance, the approach must be different because the ministers must keep in mind that it is unlike the normal church service/worship setup where there aren't too many things to concentrate on except to take the congregation into the presence of God. In the live worship, more things must be taken into consideration and, moreover, the number of ministers may be many. Also, unlike the church service set-up, special live events or programs can be organized in a multi-cultural way and can involve different languages where the people have an opportunity to praise and worship the Lord in their native languages.

It is very important to understand these differences between the church-setting praise and worship-ministration and the live praise and worship event/program.

Praise and worship in the church setting has fewer interruptions by program coordinators and fewer interactions with the audience. It mainly aims at leading the congregation before the throne of God for them to praise and worship Him. If in the church service, the worship and praise leaders make the mistake of leading the congregation in the direction of a live praise and worship event, the presence and power of God will not be experienced to its fullest.

Note that, in praise and worship, how we relate to God directly is our vertical worship, pointing upwards and how we relate to our fellow believers, is the horizontal aspect of fellowship. Praise and worship ministrations in the church setting place more emphasis on the vertical while the Live Praise and Worship Event format places additional emphasis on the horizontal.

The live praise and worship event style also focuses on God. However, additional effort is incorporated into helping the people remain lively, engaged, and to maintain their level of participation. Unlike the church setting, there are more interruptions, such as the introductions of different groups and ministers, moments of call and response from the audience, etc. It is important to note, however, that one difference between the church and the world is that even in the live praise and worship event/program, the focus is still on glorifying God and not man. Remember that the church mounts the Altar of God, while the world mounts the stage. Such an event is what they refer to as a "concert".

CHAPTER SIX

HINDRANCES AND PROBLEMS TO TRUE PRAISE AND WORSHIP

God uses praise and worship to shape the world. He uses them as tools to build His kingdom and also to destroy the kingdom of the devil. Yet, believers may often find themselves facing problems or obstacles in their praise and worship. Whenever the devil wants to attack a Christian, he attacks three areas of their life that bring the joy of the Lord; their praise, their worship, and their prayer life. If he can kill the joy of the Lord within you, he can diminish your strength, for the joy of the Lord is our strength. It is for this reason that these areas are always under attack. It is the responsibility of every child of God to worship God through His son Jesus Christ and His precious blood. Above all, anyone who has been called to serve in the praise and worship ministry must always have the following qualities or else, they will be oppressed by Satan and will quickly die.

They must:

- Love the Lord and have a heart for praise and worship
- Be a true worshipper of God and not of men
- Have a yearning to lead the Lord's people into His presence

Some practical tips to prevent the devil from hindering praise and worship (Obstacles to praise and worship)

1. **Beware of Satan**: Satan will oppose us for the mere reason that we desire to organize the praise and worship ministry and for all the reasons that we wish to worship God. Rest assured that, if you are making progress, he will intensify his attempts to distract you. It's therefore crucial that you pray for protection for yourself, your family, and for those who are close to you. You must also remember to pray for others who are involved in building the praise and the worship ministry. Praise and worship provokes Satan; and our prayer, by the power of His Spirit, is our best defense.

2. **Watch over the gift and vision:** Satan hates worshippers of Yahweh because he once fell from the very position which they hold. Therefore, you must be watchful. Study to show yourself approved and able to watch over the gift and the vision and so that the devil doesn't steal, kill, or destroy it.

3. **Don't allow other church activities to overshadow the time of true praise and worship**: The amount of activities that the church can accomplish is not a threat to Satan. It is the effectiveness of what we do that threatens his kingdom. True and effective praise and worship will advance the work of God. Since Satan cannot stop praise and worship nor stand its power, he will attempt to pollute it.

4. **Do not exclude God from your ministry**: You must always allow God to move in all that you do, especially in your praise and worship sessions. If you meet regularly as a praise and worship team to pray for the needs of the congregation, and for God's grace to usher them into God's presence through your ministrations, then you have already successfully implemented a very crucial portion of the music ministry.

5. **Watch out for pride**: Remember that Satan (then called Lucifer) was good at worship; but pride, greed, and arrogance brought him down. Therefore, it will be very wise for the leaders and the entire music ministry to humble themselves for God to uplift them.

6. **Keep your appointment with God:** Another hindrance to praise and worship is the lack of proper time management. Whenever you make an agreement with someone to meet with them at a specific place and time every day and you fail to show up, even for one day, you must consider how that person would feel or what they would think. In the same way, keeping our appointment with God strengthens our relationship with God and causes you to always be in His heart. The musicians, the Levites, and the priests in charge of worship in the older days developed that relationship with God when they remained at their post. They became vessels and friends with God because they were always in fellowship with the Lord. When you keep your appointment with God, and diligently honor it, He will always come to meet you because of that appointment. What I mean is, if you

respect God in your time of prayer, Bible studies, and worship, His heart will always be after you because you keep your appointment with Him.

7. **Satan limits most Christians to the Outer Court, causing them to become "Outer Court-worshippers"**: Most people in the church, even the church as a whole, have been confined to worship in the Outer Court despite the fact that the blood of Jesus has made a way for us to enter into the Holy of Holies. Most congregations are still "Outer Court-worshippers" because these people, although they are in the church, refuse to honor the time of worship. They have yet to enter through the blood because of their poor relationship with the Lord (Yahweh) and because of how they treat the blood that paved a way for us to enter into His presence, and they treat the Eternal Holy Spirit, our helper, without regard. They are ignorant about the work of the blood of Jesus Christ and the Eternal Holy Spirit.

"Hebrews 10:18-29 (KJV) Now where remission of these is, there is no more offering for sin.19 Having therefore, brethren, boldness to enter into the holies by the blood of Jesus, {boldness: or, liberty} 20 By a new and living way, which he hath consecrated for us, through the veil, that is to say, his flesh; {consecrated: or, new made} 21 And having an high priest over the house of God; 22 Let us draw near with a true heart in full assurance of faith, having our hearts sprinkled from an evil conscience, and our bodies washed with pure water. 23 Let us hold fast the profession of our faith without wavering; (for he is faithful that promised;)24 And let us consider one

another to provoke unto love and to good works: 25 Not forsaking the assembling of ourselves together, as the manner of some is; but exhorting one another: and so much the more, as ye see the day approaching. 26 For if we sin wilfully after that we have received the knowledge of the truth, there remaineth no more sacrifice for sins, 27 But a certain fearful looking for of judgment and fiery indignation, which shall devour the adversaries. 28 He that despised Moses' law died without mercy under two or three witnesses: 29 Of how much sorer punishment, suppose ye, shall he be thought worthy, who hath trodden under foot the Son of God, and hath counted the blood of the covenant, wherewith he was sanctified, an unholy thing, and hath done despite unto the Spirit of grace?"

Friends, it is a terrible thing for the church to continue to worship in the Outer Court after Christ Jesus has shed His blood. In the land of worship, where there is an abundance of the fullness of the Godhead (the Father, Eternal Holy Spirit, the Lord Jesus, the precious Blood of Jesus, and the Name of Jesus), why must we continue to live like poor beggars? Must we act and put on a performance in praise and worship without seeing His glory? Are you part of the worshippers failing God today, after all of the provisions He has made?

8. **Distractions of technology (mobile devices, etc.)**: Today, the devil is using cell phones, tablets, etc. to disrupt worship and praise in the gatherings of the saints and in churches where there is no discipline. This lack of reverence for the Lord has grown to the extent that it is during the time of praise and worship that unassigned people move about with their tablets and phones, attending to calls, text messages, interacting on social media, surfing the web, playing games, and taking pictures and videos. These behaviors can even be seen among some pastors. It disrupts and corrupts the sacred time with God.

9. **Excessive trading in the House of God:** The temple must be cleansed. Excessive commerce (buying, selling, and money changing, etc.) is going on in the House of the Lord. Just as the Lord Jesus saw them doing, and cast them out, overturning their tables and cleansing the temple, the children of God today are still attending to their own businesses in the house and work of the Lord. People have found for themselves different uses for the house of the Lord

other than the purpose for which Yahweh established His temple.

Mt21.12-13 "And Jesus went into the temple of God, and cast out all them that sold and bought in the temple, and overthrew the tables of the moneychangers, and the seats of them that sold doves, 13And said unto them, It is written, My house shall be called the house of prayer; but ye have made it a den of thieves."

Isa56:7 "these I will bring to my holy mountain and give them joy in my house of prayer. Their burnt offerings and sacrifices will be accepted on my altar; for my house will be called a house of prayer for all nations."

Jeremiah 7:11 "Has this house, which bears my Name, become a den of robbers to you? But I have been watching! Declares the LORD. It's Time to clean",

An excerpt from "Fresh Manna", by Bishop Dr. Emmanuel D. Apau Jr.

Friends, only true worshippers will be qualified on the last day. Are you part of the true worshippers? Do you know that everything will come to an end and that God will judge all things by His Word, the Gospel? (Romans 2.16).

There is a serious need for us to be knowledgeable about:

- The true and biblical teaching about the Apocalypse, the end of the World (Mat24)
- The sudden change of the saints and the raising up of the dead in Christ to be caught up in the air to be with the Lord (The Rapture, 1Thess4.15-17)
- The reign of the Antichrist, the Lawless one (Dan7.25; 2Thes 2.3,8,9,)
- The coming Great Tribulation-period (Mt24.21)
- The Armageddon War (Rev16.12-21)
- The Coming of the Lord Jesus Christ to save His nation, Israel and the saints (Zech12; Rev19.7-21)
- Christ's millennial rule on the earth with His saints (Rev20.6)
- The imprisonment of Satan's and his demons' and his short release (Rev20)
- The great white throne judgment, the judgment for all who have rejected God's call to salvation (Rev20.11-15)
- The eternal judgment, the lake of fire (Rev20.15)
- The ultimate defeat and judgment of Satan (the beast), Antichrist and death (Rev20.10and1Cor15.26), and Eternal Life-Heaven (Rev21)

Stay on your guard.

CHAPTER SEVEN

WHAT YOU CAN DO TO BUILD A STRONG AND BETTER PRAISE AND WORSHIP TEAM

The following points can help you to build your worship and praise team if you follow them very well:

1. Enroll your music ministry as a whole in special classes.
2. Participate in music workshops and seminars for praise and worship.
3. Establish a weekly rehearsal time to prepare ahead of your ministrations.
4. Teach the team, from the pastoral level, to reach the congregation.
5. Refrain from attempting to tackle too many goals at once as a team. Doing so will cause people to become overwhelmed by the many changes and it may stress out your resources (time, money, the interest of the people, etc.) as well. It is much better to begin one or two new things at a time and allow them to become established before including additional activities. For example, you must not hold too many music programs within a short period of time as it may drain people's ability to support. Also, don't tackle too many new songs at once during a practice session as it may overwhelm the musicians and vocalists.
6. Build leaders: In the music ministry, you must know that no single individual can successfully conduct a multifaceted ministry. The leader must recruit,

encourage, mentor and delegate power to others, encourage them, and promote specialization which will lead to enhanced results. You must raise more leaders and have a different person in charge of each activity. That way, you are not as likely to burn anyone out. People are more likely to do a better job when they have a sense of ownership over the job. A good leader must learn how to say NO to additional tasks before it becomes too much.

7. Not everyone will be able to participate in every activity. Not every ministry is right for everyone and not everyone may be able to participate in several ministries at once nor take part in every form of ministration. Even within the music ministry, not every song may be suitable for every member of the team to lead. Also, do not expect your leaders to take part in every activity. Each person, led by the Lord, must do what is right for them. Do not be surprised nor discouraged by who does or does not participate in every activity but rejoice and thank the Lord for those who He directs to be involved in the activity. Teach and encourage them, then allow them to participate willingly so that they can offer true worship to the Lord.

8. Keep everyone informed: To maintain enthusiasm and motivation among your team, you must be sure to update everyone on the team about the group's goals, progress, and achievements. You cannot expect the members of the team to remain motivated to reach the goals when they are not given a proper perspective of their current status and progress. Use all available avenues to inform the members of the

team and congregation as a whole about the doings of the Lord amongst you.

9. Not everyone is at the same maturity level: Not all will grow at the same rate, nor even as a result of the same stimulus. So do not forget, or else you will face many problems in your music ministry.

10. Document all rules and regulations that will guide the group to function effectively and efficiently.

11. Do not allow new people to join without first sitting down with them to explain the membership requirements of the group. Ensure that the new person has the time to attend rehearsals and can come to church as early as it is required of all the musicians and vocalists. They must be prepared to show the same level of commitment that is required. Find out what the person knows and understands about music. Are they willing and ready to learn and to go through all the necessary training? Checking these things will go a long way to ensure the growth and development of your group. You will successfully prevent many unforeseen issues and avoid allowing people to join who may become a problem and hinder the progress in the entire group or team.

CHAPTER EIGHT

THE BENEFITS OF TRUE PRAISE AND WORSHIP

True praise and worship has an uncountable number of benefits. When the right kind of atmosphere is created for true praise and worship, the results are awesome and powerful. True praise and worship is a vehicle that brings God's presence/glory to dwell among us, His congregation. Furthermore, when the presence of the Lord fills the place, anything is possible, except sin. Below are some profound benefits of true praise and worship:

1. True praise and worship grants us access to communicate with our maker.
2. It gives us access to enter into heaven where our Lord dwells. It creates and contributes to the sweet-smelling incense (the prayers) of the saints.
3. It causes God to release judgment on the earth and in the dark world through the prayers of the saints from the heavenly altar.
4. True praise and worship causes God to be pleased with us, to appreciate us, and to love us even more for acknowledging Him as our true Lord and only Creator.
5. True praise and worship releases God's presence/glory to visit us.
6. It makes Him delighted to dwell among us.
7. When His glory/presence comes, it releases an anointing/oil/power/unction for us to perform great things.
8. When that glory comes, our efforts cease to make a difference because the Lord, through His Eternal

Spirit, takes over the work to perform what men cannot do.

9. When praise and worship ascends to God,
    - His glory/presence comes down to heal
    - Deliverance comes down unto men
    - Lives are restored
    - Breakthroughs are given
    - Hopes are regained
    - Captives are set free
    - The oppressed are released
    - Prisoners are loosed from their chains

10. Salvation comes through true praise and worship.
11. True praise and worship drives out darkness.
12. A strong atmosphere of praise and worship drives out demons and they flee.
13. It causes the Lord to renew the strength of His people.
14. It moves God to reveal His mind and secret intent to us.
15. It has the power to open every impossible door.
16. God uses our praise and worship to work miracles, things that science cannot explain.
17. God uses our praise and worship as a tool to drive out, defeat and, sometimes, even kill our wicked enemies.
18. Our praise and worship can cause God to send us angelic assistance.
19. It has the power to shake the foundations of the earth, open doors, or make a way even through rivers, the wilderness, or the sea.
20. True praise and worship can break down demonic walls like that of Jericho.

21. It is one of the ways or vehicles through which we reach God, fellowship with Him, and worship Him as our Lord and King.
22. It is our way of appreciating our Lord, thanking Him and praising Him for what He has done.
23. It is one of the fastest ways through which God releases His blessings and demonstrates His goodness unto us.
24. True praise and worship resists the devil because it draws the presence of the Godhead.
25. True praise and worship gives us the opportunity and the privilege to proclaim who He is, the God of all creation.

His presence stops the current and the flow of mighty waters

Just as Moses, a servant, and prophet of the Lord, requested for when he said that they (the Israelites) will not take a step without the presence of the Lord, all that the church needs is God's presence or glory. If the fullness of God's presence were to dwell with the church at every meeting, there would be nothing that can hinder or stand in our way. Remember that it was His presence that parted the Red Sea, the Jordan River and many more. Brethren, if there is anything that the church must pray for, it is for His presence to continue to dwell among us. If we lose His presence, we would have lost everything.

The Crossing of the Red Sea and the waters of Jordan.

Joshua 3.12-17 "Now therefore take you twelve men out of the tribes of Israel, out of every tribe a man. 13 And it shall come to pass, as soon as the soles of the feet of the priests that bear the ark of the LORD, the Lord of all the earth, shall rest in the waters of Jordan, that the waters of Jordan shall be cut off from the waters that come down from above; and they shall stand upon an heap.14 And it came to pass, when the people removed from their tents, to pass over Jordan, and the priests bearing the ark of the covenant before the people; 15 And as they that bare the ark were come unto Jordan, and the feet of the priests that bare the ark were dipped in the brim of the water, (for Jordan overfloweth all his banks all the time of harvest,) 16 That the waters which came down from above stood and rose up upon an heap very far from the city Adam, that is beside Zaretan: and those that came down toward the sea of the plain, even the salt sea, failed, and were cut off: and the people passed over right against Jericho. 17 And the priests that bare the ark of the covenant of the LORD stood firm on dry ground in the midst of Jordan, and all the Israelites passed over on dry ground, until all the people were passed clean over Jordan"

Exodus 15:8
By the blast of your nostrils the waters piled up. The surging waters stood up like a wall; the deep waters congealed in the heart of the sea.

Joshua 3:16
the water from upstream stopped flowing. It piled up in a heap a great distance away, at a town called Adam in the vicinity of Zarethan, while the water flowing down to the Sea of the Arabah (that is, the Dead Sea) was completely cut off. So the people crossed over opposite Jericho.

Joshua 4:7
tell them that the flow of the Jordan was cut off before the ark of the covenant of the LORD. When it crossed the Jordan, the waters of the Jordan were cut off. These stones are to be a memorial to the people of Israel forever."

Psalm 74:15
It was you who opened up springs and streams; you dried up the ever-flowing rivers.

Psalm 114:3
The sea looked and fled, the Jordan turned back.

Joshua 3:13
And it shall come to pass, as soon as the soles of the feet of the priests that bear the ark of the LORD, the LORD of all the earth, shall rest in the waters of

Jordan, that the waters of Jordan shall be cut off from the waters that come down from above; and they shall stand on an heap.

The benefits of dwelling in and enjoying God's presence.

What are the benefits of dwelling in the secret place of the most high-(God's presence)?
If you dwell in God's secret place or in His presence:

1. He will be your Lord and God.
2. He will be your refuge and fortress.
3. He will grant you deliverance from the snare of the fowler and from the deadly pestilence.
4. He will cover you with His feathers, and you will find refuge under His wings.
5. His faithfulness will be your shield and buckler.
6. You will not fear the terror of the night, nor the arrow that flies by day, nor the pestilence that stalks in darkness, nor the destruction that wastes at noonday.
7. A thousand may fall at your side, ten thousand at your right hand, but it will not come near you.
8. You will be able to look with your eyes and see the recompense of the wicked.
9. No evil will be allowed to befall you.
10. No plague will come near your tent.
11. He will command His angels concerning you to guard you in all your ways. On their hands, they will bear you up, lest you strike your foot against a stone.
12. You will tread on the lion and the adder; the young lion and the serpent, you will trample underfoot.

Stay in God's presence and enjoy His benefits.

Psalm91:16 (KJV). *"He that dwelleth in the secret place of the most High shall abide under the shadow of the Almighty. {abide: Heb. lodge} 2 I will say of the LORD, He is my refuge and my fortress: my God; in him will I trust. 3 Surely he shall deliver thee from the snare of the fowler, and from the noisome pestilence. 4 He shall cover thee with his feathers, and under his wings shalt thou trust: his truth shall be thy shield and buckler. 5 Thou shalt not be afraid for the terror by night; nor for the arrow that flieth by day; 6 Nor for the pestilence that walketh in darkness; nor for the destruction that wasteth at noonday. 7 A thousand shall fall at thy side, and ten thousand at thy right hand; but it shall not come nigh thee. 8 Only with thine eyes shalt thou behold and see the reward of the wicked. 9 Because thou hast made the LORD, which is my refuge, even the most High, thy habitation; 10 There shall no evil befall thee, neither shall any plague come nigh thy dwelling. 11 For he shall give his angels charge over thee, to keep thee in all thy ways. 12 They shall bear thee up in their hands, lest thou dash thy foot against a stone. 13 Thou shalt tread upon the lion and adder: the young lion and the dragon shalt thou trample under feet. {adder: or, asp} 14 Because he hath set his love upon me, therefore will I deliver him: I will set him on high, because he hath known my name. 15 He shall call upon me, and I will answer him: I will be with him in trouble; I will deliver him, and honour him. 16 Withlong life will I satisfy him, and shew him my salvation. {Long...: Heb. length of days}"*.

__Exodus 33:22__ *"When my glory passes by, I will put you in a cleft in the rock and cover you with my hand until I have passed by".*

__Psalm 17:8__ *"Keep me as the apple of your eye; hide me in the shadow of your wings"*

__Psalm 27:5__ *"For in the day of trouble he will keep me safe in his dwelling; he will hide me in the shelter of his sacred tent and set me high upon a rock"*

__Psalm 31:20__ *"In the shelter of your presence you hide them from all human intrigues; you keep them safe in your dwelling from accusing tongues"*

__Psalm 32:7__ *"You are my hiding place; you will protect me from trouble and surround me with songs of deliverance".*

__Psalm 90:1__ *"A prayer of Moses the man of God. Lord, you have been our dwelling place throughout all generations"*

The Benefits of dwelling in God's Presence

Those who dwell in the presence of God are like a well-watered garden; Living Water flows through them. They will experience and see the following signs:

1. They will be like a tree planted by rivers.

2. They will bring forth their fruit in season.
3. Their leaves will not wither.
4. They will prosper in whatsoever they do.

> ***Psalm1.1-6 (KJV)*** *Blessed is the man that walketh not in the counsel of the ungodly, nor standeth in the way of sinners, nor sitteth in the seat of the scornful. {ungodly: or, wicked} 2But his delight is in the law of the LORD; and in his law doth he meditate day and night. 3And he shall be like a tree planted by the rivers of water, that bringeth forth his fruit in his season; his leaf also shall not wither; and whatsoever he doeth shall prosper. {wither: Heb. fade} 4The ungodly are not so: but are like the chaff which the wind driveth away. 5Therefore the ungodly shall not stand in the judgment, nor sinners in the congregation of the righteous. 6For the LORD knoweth the way of the righteous: but the way of the ungodly shall perish. May The LORD guide you always;*

Prayer 1

May the Lord satisfy your needs by watering you when you are dry and restoring your strength. May He give strength to your bones. May He cause you to be like a well-watered garden and like a spring of water whose waters do not fail. May Yahweh water you, both spiritually and physically. May the water that He gives become, within you, a well of water springing up into everlasting life.

> ***John 4:14*** *but whoever drinks the water I give them will never thirst. Indeed, the water I give them will*

become in them a spring of water welling up to eternal life."

John 4:10 *Jesus answered her, "If you knew the gift of God and who it is that asks you for a drink, you would have asked him and he would have given you living water."*

John 7:38 *whoever believes in me, as Scripture has said, rivers of living water will flow from within them."*

Isaiah 55:1 *Come, all you who are thirsty, come to the waters; and you who have no money, come, buy and eat! Come, buy wine and milk without money and without cost.*

Isaiah 58.11b *you will be like a well-watered garden, like a spring whose waters never fail.*

There is nothing more beautiful and glorious than to see the presence/glory of the Lord filling His temple and taking over the atmosphere to a point where the priests and the workers in the temple can no longer stand to perform their duties. It is in such an environment that you can see and witness Him move supernaturally. Fellow believers, it has happened before, and it can happen again. We can witness lives touched, souls saved, the sick healed, the oppressed and prisoners set free. If only the church will give God true worship, His glory will come down to perform mighty things in our midst.

Prayer 2

May God fill His temple with His presence again.
All that the church needs is His glory.

Where is the glory of the Lord and how can it come into our midst?

2Ch 5:13-14 It came even to pass, as the trumpeters and singers were as one, to make one sound to be heard in praising and thanking the LORD; and when they lifted up their voice with the trumpets and cymbals and instruments of musick, and praised the LORD, saying, For he is good; for his mercy endureth for ever: that then the house was filled with a cloud, even the house of the LORD; (14) So that the priests could not stand to minister by reason of the cloud: for the glory of the LORD had filled the house of God.

Exo40:35 Moses could not enter the tent of meeting because the cloud had settled on it, and the glory of the LORD filled the tabernacle;

1Kng 8:11 And the priests could not perform their service because of the cloud, for the glory of the LORD filled his temple;

2Chro7:2 The priests could not enter the temple of the LORD because the glory of the LORD filled it;

When God's glory fully takes over, men are even granted rest. The presence of God is the only one that can satisfy the church and give peace and rest to His people.

Seeking the Lord's Presence in our worship with all our hearts

When people's hearts go after signs and wonders without first seeking the presence of the giver, they ultimately miss both; but when they first seek the giver and His presence or glory, all the other things follow or are added. Folks, let us seek the LORD and His strength; seek His presence continually and He will Shepherd your life...

Ps105.4 Seek the LORD, and His strength: seek His face evermore;

Ps23.5 You prepare a table before me in the presence of my enemies; You have anointed my head with oil; My cup overflows. 6Surely goodness and mercy shall follow me all the days of my life: and I will dwell in the house of the LORD forever.

Mt6:33"But seek first His kingdom and His righteousness, and all these things will be added to you.

34"So do not worry about tomorrow; for tomorrow will care for itself. Each day has enough trouble of its own;

1Tim4:8For physical training is of some value, but godliness has value for all things, holding promise for both the present life and the life to come.

Shalom.

CHAPTER NINE

BIBLICAL SOUNDS (INSTRUMENTS)

How to use biblical instruments correctly and see results in your ministration.

2 Chronicles 5:12-13 All the Levites who were musicians--Asaph, Heman, Jeduthun and their sons and relatives--stood on the east side of the altar, dressed in fine linen and playing cymbals, harps and lyres. They were accompanied by 120 priests sounding trumpets. In unison when the trumpeters and the singers were to make themselves heard with one voice to praise and to glorify the LORD, and when they lifted up their voice accompanied by trumpets and cymbals and instruments of music, and when they praised the LORD saying, "He indeed is good for His lovingkindness is everlasting," then the house, the house of the LORD, was filled with a cloud,... And when they praised the LORD saying, "He indeed is good for His lovingkindness is everlasting," then the house, the house of the LORD, was filled with a cloud.

Biblically, certain sounds or instruments have been prescribed for the worship of the Lord and have a great impact on the service when used correctly. God demands the right instruments to be played for the proper atmosphere to be created for Him to move in our services and in His worship. Biblical sounds are powerful tools. They are a means of communication between us and our God and one of the ways for us to communicate while worshipping. Tremendous results can be seen when:

1. The congregation as a whole has one purpose, vision, and aim.
2. There is a proper song arrangement.
3. There is good communication and planning amongst the instrumentalists and vocalists. All musicians must know or be taught the right time that each instrument must be played.
4. The musicians learn the attributes of God and the types of instruments that proclaim those specific attributes of Yahweh (the Lord).
5. The musicians set themselves apart for the Lord as Holy vessels and work with the precious Holy Spirit.
6. The musicians create an atmosphere of peace, working together in a positive environment.
7. The musicians work in harmony and in unity with the Eternal Holy Spirit through the bond of peace. The musicians must know and understand that the Holy Spirit is working with them and flows only through an atmosphere of peace.

    As worshippers, we must avoid fighting, strife, tension, disorganization, disintegration, indiscipline, etc. We cannot do what we want or insist on having our way and expect to see God move in our midst.

Ephesians 4:1-13 (KJV) " *I therefore, the prisoner of the Lord, beseech you that ye walk worthy of the vocation wherewith ye are called, {of the Lord: or, in the Lord} 2With all lowliness and meekness, with longsuffering, forbearing one another in love; 3 Endeavouring to keep the unity of the Spirit in the*

Even worldly sounds have their effects and can achieve certain things when they are played; how much more do the Biblical sounds? Biblical sounds, like trumpets, cymbals, harp, lyre, etc., announce God's presence or glory, lordship, ability, worship, and creativity, and also alert the people or congregation to worship under divine instruction, etc. When the right atmosphere is created in our praise and worship, we will experience the visitation and performance of the Lord.

Psalm 150:1-6(KJV) *"Praise ye the LORD. Praise God in his sanctuary: praise him in the firmament of* *his power. {Praise ye...: Heb. Hallelujah} 2 Praise him for his mighty acts: praise him according to his excellent greatness. 3 Praise him with the sound of the trumpet: praise him with the psaltery and harp. {trumpet: or, cornet} 4 Praise him with the timbrel and dance: praise him with stringed instruments and organs. {dance: or, pipe} 5 Praise him upon the loud cymbals: praise him upon the high sounding cymbals. 6 Let everything that hath breath praise the LORD. Praise ye the LORD.*

***Psalm 144.9** I will sing a new song unto thee, O God: upon a psaltery and an instrument of ten strings will I sing praises unto thee.*

***Ps33:1-3(KJV)** "Rejoice in the LORD, O ye righteous: for praise is comely for the upright. 2 Praise the LORD with harp: sing unto him with the psaltery and an instrument of ten strings. 3 Sing unto him a new song; play skilfully with a loud noise."*

***Ps9:1-3(KJV)** "It is a good thing to give thanks unto the LORD, and to sing praises unto thy name, O most High: 2 To shew forth thy lovingkindness in the morning, and thy faithfulness every night, {every...: Heb. in the nights} 3 Upon an instrument of ten strings, and upon the psaltery; upon the harp with a solemn sound. {the harp...: or, the solemn sound with the harp} {a solemn...: Heb. Higgaion}"*

***2Sam 6:5(KJV)** "And David and all the house of Israel played before the LORD on all manner of instruments made of fir wood, even on harps, and on psalteries, and on timbrels, and on cornets, and on cymbals."*

1Chr15:13-16 (KJV). "*For because ye did it not at the first, the LORD our God made a breach upon us, for that we sought him not after the due order. 14 So the priests and the Levites sanctified themselves to bring up the ark of the LORD God of Israel. 15 And the children of the Levites bare the ark of God upon their shoulders with the staves thereon, as Moses commanded according to the word of the LORD. 16 And David spake to the chief of the Levites to appoint their brethren to be the singers with instruments of musick, psalteries and harps and cymbals, sounding, by lifting up the voice with joy.*"

2Chr 20:28 (KJV). "*And they came to Jerusalem with psalteries and harps and trumpets unto the house of the LORD.*"

Neh12:27-36(KJV). "*And at the dedication of the wall of Jerusalem they sought the Levites out of all their places, to bring them to Jerusalem, to keep the dedication with gladness, both with thanksgivings, and with singing, with cymbals, psalteries, and with harps. 28 And the sons of the singers gathered themselves together, both out of the plain country round about Jerusalem, and from the villages of Netophathi; 29 Also from the house of Gilgal, and out of the fields of Geba and Azmaveth: for the singers had builded them villages round about Jerusalem. 30 And the priests and the Levites purified themselves, and purified the people, and the gates, and the wall. 31 Then I brought up the princes of Judah upon the wall, and appointed two great companies of them that gave thanks, whereof one went on the right hand upon the wall toward the dung gate: 32 And after them went Hoshaiah, and half of the princes of Judah, 33 And Azariah, Ezra, and Meshullam, 34 Judah, and Benjamin, and Shemaiah, and Jeremiah, 35 And certain of the priests' sons with trumpets; namely, Zechariah the son of Jonathan, the son of Shemaiah, the son of Mattaniah, the son of Michaiah, the son of Zaccur, the son of Asaph: 36 And his brethren, Shemaiah, and Azarael, Milalai, Gilalai, Maai, Nethaneel, and Judah, Hanani, with the musical instruments of David the man of God, and Ezra the scribe before them."*

The purpose and effect of trumpets:
1. To awaken and for alertness.

Prayer

May the Lord sound divine trumpets through His angels to awaken your physical and spiritual man for another level of worship and service, in Jesus' name.

Isa27.13 "And it shall come to pass in that day, that the great trumpet shall be blown, and they shall come which were ready to perish in the land of Assyria, and the outcasts in the land of Egypt, and shall worship the LORD in the holy mount at Jerusalem"

Lev25:9 "Then have the trumpet sounded everywhere on the tenth day of the seventh month; on the Day of Atonement sound the trumpet throughout your land"

1Chro15:24 "Shebaniah, Joshaphat, Nethanel, Amasai, Zechariah, Benaiah & Eliezer the priests were to blow trumpets before the ark of God. Obed-

Edom and Jehiah were also to be doorkeepers for the ark;

Rev11:15 *The seventh angel sounded his trumpet, and there were loud voices in heaven, which said: "The kingdom of the world has become the kingdom of our Lord and of his Messiah, and he will reign for ever & ever.".*

The purpose and effect of trumpets:
2. For warning, to remind, and to bring vigilance.

May God use the trumpets of the watchmen - (the ministers and angels) to warn and alert us so that nothing evil takes us by surprise.

Ezekiel 33:2-4 *"Son of man, speak to the sons of your people and say to them, 'If I bring a sword upon a land, and the people of the land take one man from among them and make him their watchman, 3and he sees the sword coming upon the land and blows on the trumpet and warns the people, 4then he who hears the sound of the trumpet and does not take warning, and a sword comes and takes him away, his blood will be on his own head.*

Hosea 8:1 *"Put the trumpet to your lips! An eagle is over the house of the LORD because the people have broken my covenant and rebelled against my law.*

Amos 3:6 *"When a trumpet sounds in a city, do not the people tremble? When disaster comes to a city, has not the LORD caused it?"*

***Zephaniah 1.16** "A day of the trumpet and alarm against the fenced cities, and against the high towers"*

The purpose and effect of trumpets:
3. To call to obedience, for warning, and for preparation.

Obey the sound of the trumpet for it will prepare you to meet our soon coming King.

Prayer

May the Lord use trumpets to get the attention of His people, to prepare them, and to position them for His coming. May Yahweh, the Lord, blow the trumpet through His holy angels and prepare you for His second coming.

***Joel 2:1** Blow the trumpet in Zion; sound the alarm on my holy hill. Let all who live in the land tremble, for the day of the LORD is coming. It is close at hand—*

***Joel 2:11** The LORD thunders at the head of his army; his forces are beyond number, and mighty is the army that obeys his command. The day of the LORD is great; it is dreadful. Who can endure it?*

***Obadiah 1:15** "The day of the LORD is near for all nations. As you have done, it will be done to you; your deeds will return upon your own head.*

***Zephaniah 1:14** The great day of the LORD is near- - and coming quickly. The cry on the day of the LORD is bitter; the Mighty Warrior shouts his battle cry.*

His coming is at hand, so do not ignore the sound of the trumpet. Shalom!

1 Corinthians 14:7 Even in the case of lifeless things that make sounds, such as the pipe or harp, how will anyone know what tune is being played unless there is a distinction in the notes? 8For if the trumpet give an uncertain sound, who shall prepare himself to the battle?

Numbers 10:7 To gather the assembly, blow the trumpets, but not with the signal for setting out.

Jeremiah 4:5 "Announce in Judah and proclaim in Jerusalem and say: 'Sound the trumpet throughout the land!' Cry aloud and say: 'Gather together! Let us flee to the fortified cities!'

Ezekiel 33:3 and he sees the sword coming against the land and blows the trumpet to warn the people,

Hosea 5:8 "Sound the trumpet in Gibeah, the horn in Ramah. Raise the battle cry in Beth Aven; lead on, Benjamin.

Joel 2:15 Blow the trumpet in Zion, declare a holy fast, call a sacred assembly.

Zephaniah 1:16a day of trumpet and battle cry against the fortified cities and against the corner towers.

Revelation 8:2 And I saw the seven angels who stand before God, and seven trumpets were given to them.

Revelation 11:15 The seventh angel sounded his trumpet, and there were loud voices in heaven, which said: "The kingdom of the world has become the kingdom of our Lord and of his Messiah, and he will reign for ever and ever.

__Numbers 10:9__ When you go into battle in your own land against an enemy who is oppressing you, sound a blast on the trumpets. Then you will be remembered by the LORD your God and rescued from your enemies.

The purpose and effect of trumpets:
4. For a shout-offering, to call for steps of faith, to command, to give direction.

Trumpets and shouts: When the people gave a shout offering unto the Lord, the priest announced God's presence through the trumpets, giving Yahweh true praise and worship and this caused the walls of the city of Jericho to come down.

You must learn how to give a shout offering.

__Josh6:4-21__"Also seven priests shall carry seven trumpets of rams' horns before the ark; then on the seventh day you shall march around the city seven times, and the priests shall blow the trumpets.5"It shall be that when they make a long blast with the ram's horn, and when you hear the sound of the trumpet, all the people shall shout with a great shout; and the wall of the city will fall down flat, and the people will go up every man straight ahead."20So the people shouted, and priests blew the trumpets; and when the people heard the sound of the trumpet, the people shouted with a great shout and the wall fell down flat, so that the people went up into the city, every man straight ahead, and they took the city.

21They utterly destroyed everything in the city, both man and woman, young and old, and ox and sheep and donkey, with the edge of the sword.

Give God a shout of praise by faith with the sound of a trumpet and the walls in your life (hindrances, obstacles, the things trying to prevent you from reaching your destination) will fall down flat.

Take your position and praise God

Do you want God's glory to fill His temple once again? Then let the priests, the Levites, the singers, and the congregation take their positions to present proper worship as it is prescribed by the Lord. Let them use biblical instruments to draw the glory.

> *2Chro7.6 The priests took their assigned positions, and so did the Levites who were singing, "His faithful love endures forever!" They accompanied the singing with music from the instruments King David had made for praising the LORD. Across from the Levites, the priests blew the trumpets, while all Israel stood*

> *1Chronicles 15:16 David told the leaders of the Levites to appoint their fellow Levites as musicians to make a joyful sound with musical instruments: lyres, harps and cymbals.*

> *1 Chronicles 16:42 Heman and Jeduthun were responsible for the sounding of the trumpets and cymbals and for the playing of the other instruments*

for sacred song. The sons of Jeduthun were stationed at the gate.

2 Chronicles 5:12-13 All the Levites who were musicians--Asaph, Heman, Jeduthun and their sons and relatives--stood on the east side of the altar, dressed in fine linen and playing cymbals, harps and lyres. They were accompanied by 120 priests sounding trumpets. 13in unison when the trumpeters and the singers were to make themselves heard with one voice to praise and to glorify the LORD, and when they lifted up their voice accompanied by trumpets and cymbals and instruments of music, and when they praised the LORD saying, "He indeed is good for His lovingkindness is everlasting," then the house, the house of the LORD, was filled with a cloud,... And when they praised the LORD saying, "He indeed is good for His loving kindness is everlasting," then the house, the house of the LORD, was filled with a cloud,

Prayer

May you remain at your post to worship and praise Him for the rest of your life that you may see the performance of Jehovah God in Jesus' mighty name, amen, and amen. Shalom.

2 Chronicles 7:5 And King Solomon offered a sacrifice of twenty-two thousand head of cattle and a hundred and twenty thousand sheep and goats. So the king and all the people dedicated the temple of God.

Creating an atmosphere that invites the Spirit of the Lord.

An Atmosphere:
An atmosphere, in this case, is a process whereby the appropriate instruments, word of exaltation, and vocals in the worship and praise of our Lord are used to create a spiritual environment that is very appealing, conducive, and welcoming to the Spirit of the Lord and will cause God's glory or presence to dwell in the midst of His people. There are several ways to create this kind of atmosphere for the move of the Lord depending on the will of God, the purpose of the gathering, the expectation of the people, their preparation, and their approach to worship and praise. When all these are done well and in a way that pleases the Lord, He releases His Smoke or causes His Glory or Presence to fill the room. In such a moment, miracles can occur.

An atmosphere of worship and praise that brings healing and deliverance

Creating a powerful atmosphere with music plays a major role in the healing and deliverance ministry. Anytime praise and worship ascends and is accepted by God, His presence (or glory) comes down. When His presence comes down amidst His church, it produces the anointing (the unction, oil or power) that brings healing, deliverance, restoration, wholeness, etc. Therefore, there is a need to create an atmosphere that pleases the Lord and fits the occasion and one that will cause God to act for the benefit of His people.

The vocalists and instrumentalists

The ministry of true gospel singers and instrumentalists:

God has given the divine and spiritual responsibility of creating an atmosphere for His service and worship to the vocalists and instrumentalists.

The Lord, through King David the worshipper and the commanders of the army, appointed certain individuals to be vocalists and instrumentalists in the temple (1 Chronicles 25:1,6-7). To prophesy, in this scriptural context, means to speak the mind of God with great earnestness and devout affections under the influence of the Eternal Holy Spirit of the Lord.

1 Chronicles 15:16 David told the leaders of the Levites to appoint their fellow Levites as musicians to make a joyful sound with musical instruments: lyres, harps and cymbals.

1 Chronicles 16:41 With them were Heman and Jeduthun and the rest of those chosen and designated by name to give thanks to the LORD, "for his love endures forever."

2 Chronicles 5:12 All the Levites who were musicians-- Asaph, Heman, Jeduthun and their sons and relatives--stood on the east side of the altar, dressed in fine linen and playing cymbals, harps and lyres. They were accompanied by 120 priests sounding trumpets.

2 Chronicles 34:12 The workers labored faithfully. Over them to direct them were Jahath and Obadiah, Levites descended from Merari, and Zechariah and Meshullam, descended from Kohath.

The Levites who were skilled in playing musical instruments, etc., fulfilled their appointment faithfully.

CHAPTER TEN

SATANIC WORSHIP (666)

Another kingdom, apart from the kingdom of God, is Satan's kingdom. Its teachings and practices are from Satan, the head of all the fallen angels that fell with a third of the stars. He was the Archangel, then called Lucifer, who fell from his position. Just as God's kingdom has its way of worship, likewise, Satan's kingdom has its own kind of worship. Satan's kingdom also uses music as a means of communication with their gods. Unlike the kingdom of the Lord which has only one God, the satanic kingdom involves the worship of several gods and it is the fallen angels who work behind all these to promote their master's work and kingdom. In their worship of Satan, music is one of the powerful tools that they use to communicate with their gods and amongst themselves. Their songs mostly involve insults, blasphemy, profanity and many more which are able to attract and win souls for Satan, especially the youth, to divert their attention from the one and only true God.

The spirit behind all satanic worship is the spirit of the Antichrist. That spirit hates Christ and for that reason works in so many ways to oppose godly worship. At times, in their gatherings and festivals, the spirit of the antichrist from Satan manifests among them. God, through His word, has warned us repeatedly about this spirit of the world which blinds people and prevents them from seeing the light. Very soon, this spirit, called the Antichrist spirit from Satan, will be made manifest in a physical being, taking full possession of a man, to finish Satan's end-time assignment. He will introduce, what the Lord, through His word and by the Apostle John, describes as the mark of the beast, 666. This spirit is already at work in this world, using many people, churches, kings, presidents, judges, scientists, doctors, lawyers, pastors, and so on, who are waiting for the period of His manifestation in the flesh.

NOTE: To read more about Satanic and Demonic Worship, please read "Demonology and Breaking of Curses" by Bishop Dr. Emmanuel D. Apau Jr.

Be alert and aware of satanic worship

The worship of Satan (666):

Do you know that the time is coming, and it is coming quickly, when God will permit worshippers of Satan and fake religion to force all men to worship Satan and those who refuse to worship him will be killed?

Rev13:12-16 "It exercised all the authority of the first beast on its behalf, and made the earth and its inhabitants worship the first beast, whose fatal wound had been healed. And it performed great signs, even causing fire to come down from heaven to the earth in full view of the people. Because of the signs it was given power to perform on behalf of the first beast, it deceived the inhabitants of the earth. It ordered them to set up an image in honor of the beast who was wounded by the sword and yet lived. The second beast was given power to give breath to the image of the first beast, so that the image could speak and cause all who refused to worship the image to be killed. It also forced all people, great and small, rich and poor, free and slave, to receive a mark on their right hands or on their foreheads."

Folks, now is the time to serve God faithfully and to make sure you don't miss the rapture. For only true believers shall be raptured (the catching up of the saints in the clouds to meet with the Lord in the air). Shalom.

The mark of the beast (666)

Do you know that, very soon, God will allow Satan to establish a one-world government? And without the mark, 666, none can buy nor sell?

Rev13.16 and he causes all, the small and the great, and the rich and the poor, and the free men and the slaves, to be given a mark on their right hand or on their forehead, 17and he provides that no one will be able to buy or to sell, except the one who has the mark, either the name of the beast or the number of his name. 18Here is wisdom. Let him who has understanding calculate the number of the beast, for the number is that of a man; and his number is six hundred and sixty-six;

14:9A third angel followed them and said in a loud voice: "If anyone worships the beast and its image and receives its mark on their forehead or on their hand. 11And the smoke of their torment will rise for ever and ever. There will be no rest day or night for those who worship the beast and its image, or for anyone who receives the mark of its name." Folks, let's serve god faithfully, and be positioned for god's seal before its late-Rev7:3"do not harm the land or the sea or the trees until we put a seal on the foreheads of the servants of our God." Gal6:17From now on, let no one cause me trouble, for I bear on my body the marks of Jesus. Watch out, for the times are evil, shalom.

Satan and the antichrist shall kill the saints who fail to worship him when the spirit of the antichrist manifests in flesh, but God will resurrect them all.

They will behead many for testifying about Jesus and for refusing to worship the beast and take the mark, 666. However, God will cause them to gain endless life in the first resurrection.

Rev20:4I saw thrones on which were seated those who had been given authority to judge. And I saw the souls of those who had been beheaded because of their testimony about Jesus and because of the word of God. They had not worshiped the beast or its image and had not received its mark on their foreheads or their hands. They came to life and reigned with Christ a thousand years. 5 The rest of the dead did not come to life until the thousand years were ended. This is the first resurrection. 6 Blessed and holy is the one who shares in the first resurrection! Over such the second death has no power, but they will be priests of God and of Christ, and they will reign with him for a thousand years.

Rev13.15And he had power to give life unto the image of the beast, that the image of the beast should both speak, and cause that as many as would not worship the image of the beast should be killed.

Stand in the faith, for hard times are coming, shalom.

The final destination of the beast, the false prophets, the antichrist, and their followers.

Yahweh will command His angels to release the bowls of His judgment upon the beast, the false prophets, and those that worship it. The beast will be captured, his throne will be defeated, and all who worshiped him will weep eternally.

Rev16.8And the fourth angel poured out his vial upon the sun; and power was given unto him to scorch men with fire.9And men were scorched with great heat, and blasphemed the name of God, which hath power over these plagues: and they repented not to give him glory.10And the fifth angel poured out his vial upon the seat of the beast; and his kingdom was full of darkness; and they gnawed their tongues for pain,

Rev19:20But the beast was captured, and with it the false prophet who had performed the signs on its behalf. With these signs he had deluded those who had received the mark of the beast and worshiped its image. The two of them were thrown alive into the fiery lake of burning sulfur.

Shalom.

Antichrist and his followers shall be destroyed, but those who die for their faith in Christ will regain their lives.

2Thess2:7-9 "For the mystery of lawlessness is already at work; only he who now restrains will do so until he is taken out of the way. Then that lawless one will be revealed whom the Lord will slay with the breath of His mouth and bring to an end by the appearance of His coming; that is, the one whose coming is in accord with the activity of Satan, with all power and signs and false wonders,..."

Revelation 20:4I saw thrones on which were seated those who had been given authority to judge. And I saw the souls of those who had been beheaded because of their testimony about Jesus and because of the word of God. They had not worshiped the beast or its image and had not received its mark on their foreheads or their hands. They came to life and reigned with Christ a thousand years;

Revelation 16:2The first angel went and poured out his bowl on the land, and ugly, festering sores broke out on the people who had the mark of the beast and worshiped its image;

Revelation 16:2 The first angel went and poured out his bowl on the land, and ugly, festering sores broke out on the people who had the mark of the beast and worshiped its image.

The spirit of the Antichrist and the false prophets is at work:

Many people claim to know God. There is an uncountable number who even profess to know Jesus Christ as their Lord and personal savior and, yet, deny Him by their works and by the way they live. There are many counterfeit churches, believers and faith, especially in these last days. A majority even fail to live genuine Christian lives. Most people profess their faith based on superficial emotions and not on the power of the Holy Spirit nor on having faith in God's Holy Word. Many are in the church but are being deceived and have counterfeit faith. They may feel saved but continue to lose the battle of sin and still cling to their old ways.

> ***Titus 1.6*** *They profess to know God, but they deny him by their works. They are detestable, disobedient, unfit for any good work.*

> ***2Tim 3.5*** *"holding to a form of godliness, although they have denied its power; Avoid such men as these". The spirit of Antichrist & false prophets is busy working even in most churches using a lot of people.*

Watch out, for Christ's second coming is near and the devil is more desperate for souls than before.

CHAPTER ELEVEN

CONCLUSION

We must understand that our worship unto the Lord and King will not end here. As true worshippers, we will worship God even better in the world to come, for Yahweh (the Lord) deserves to be worshipped both now and forever. Our God collapsed the great wall of Jericho in the old days through Joshua and the Israelites' worship and praise.

Joshua6.1-27 Now Jericho was straitly shut up because of the children of Israel: none went out, and none came in. {was…: Heb. did shut up, and was shut up} 2 And the LORD said unto Joshua, See, I have given into thine hand Jericho, and the king thereof, and the mighty men of valour. 3 And ye shall compass the city, all ye men of war, and go round about the city once. Thus shalt thou do six days. 4 And seven priests shall bear before the ark seven trumpets of rams' horns: and the seventh day ye shall compass the city seven times, and the priests shall blow with the trumpets. 5 And it shall come to pass, that when they make a long blast with the ram's horn, and when ye hear the sound of the trumpet, all the people shall shout with a great shout; and the wall of the city shall fall down flat, and the people shall ascend up every man straight before him. {flat: Heb. under it} 6 And Joshua the son of Nun called the priests, and said unto them, Take up the ark of the covenant, and let seven priests bear seven trumpets of rams' horns before the ark of the LORD. 7 And he said unto the people, Pass on, and compass the city, and let him that is armed pass on before the ark of the LORD. 8 And it came to pass, when Joshua had spoken unto the people, that the seven priests bearing the seven trumpets of rams' horns passed on before the LORD, and blew with the trumpets: and the ark of the covenant of the LORD followed them. 9 And the armed men went before the priests that blew with the trumpets, and the rereward came after the ark, the priests going on, and blowing with the trumpets. {rereward: Heb. gathering host} 10 And Joshua had commanded the people, saying, Ye shall not shout, nor make any noise with your voice, neither shall any word proceed out of your mouth, until the day I bid you shout; then shall ye shout. {any noise...: Heb. your voice to be heard} 11 So the ark of the LORD compassed the city, going about it once: and they came into the camp, and lodged in the camp. 12 And Joshua rose early in the morning, and the priests took up the ark of the LORD. 13 And seven priests bearing seven trumpets of rams' horns before the ark of the LORD went on continually, and blew with the trumpets: and the armed men went before them; but the rereward came after the ark of the LORD, the priests going on, and blowing with the trumpets. 14 And the second day they compassed the city once, and returned into the camp: so they did six days. 15 And it came to pass on the seventh day, that they rose early about the dawning of the day, and compassed the city after the same manner seven times: only on that day they compassed the city seven times. 16 And it came to pass at the seventh time, when the priests blew with the trumpets, Joshua said unto the people, Shout; for the LORD hath given you the city.17 And the city shall be accursed, even it, and all that are therein, to the LORD: only Rahab the harlot shall live, she and all that are with her in the house, because she hid the messengers that we sent. {accursed: or, devoted} 18 And ye, in any wise keep yourselves from the accursed thing, lest ye make yourselves accursed, when ye take of the accursed thing, and make the camp of Israel a curse, and trouble it. {accursed: or, devoted} {a curse: or, devoted} 19 But all the silver, and gold, and vessels of brass and iron, are consecrated unto the LORD: they shall come into the treasury of the LORD. {consecrated: Heb. holiness} 20 So the people shouted when the priests blew with the trumpets: and it came to pass, when the people heard the sound of the trumpet, and the people shouted with a great shout, that the wall fell down flat, so that the people went up into the city, every man straight before him, and they took the city. {flat: Heb. under it} 21 And they utterly destroyed all that was in the city, both man and woman, young and old, and ox, and sheep, and ass, with the edge of the sword. 22 But Joshua had said unto the two men that had spied out the country, Go into the harlot's house, and bring out thence the woman, and all that she hath, as ye sware unto her. 23 And the young men that were spies went in, and brought out Rahab, and her father, and her mother, and her brethren, and all that she had; and they brought out all her kindred, and left them without the camp of Israel. {kindred: Heb. families} 24 And they burnt the city with fire, and all that was therein: only the silver, and the gold, and the vessels of brass and of iron, they put into the treasury of the house of the LORD. 25 And Joshua saved Rahab the harlot alive, and her father's household, and all that she had; and she dwelleth in Israel even unto this day; because she hid the messengers, which Joshua sent to spy out Jericho. 26 And Joshua adjured them at that time, saying, Cursed be the man before the LORD, that riseth up and buildeth this city Jericho: he shall lay the foundation thereof in his firstborn, and in his youngest son shall he set up the gates of it. 27So the LORD was with Joshua; and his fame was noised throughout all the country;

God used Jehoshaphat to defeat nations through the power of praise and worship.

2Chronicles 20.1-37 It came to pass after this also, that the children of Moab, and the children of Ammon, and with them other beside the Ammonites, came against Jehoshaphat to battle. 2 Then there came some that told Jehoshaphat, saying, There cometh a great multitude against thee from beyond the sea on this side Syria; and, behold, they be in Hazazontamar, which is Engedi. 3 And Jehoshaphat feared, and set himself to seek the LORD, and proclaimed a fast throughout all Judah. {himself: Heb. his face} 4 And Judah gathered themselves together, to ask help of the LORD: even out of all the cities of Judah they came to seek the LORD. 5And Jehoshaphat stood in the congregation of Judah and Jerusalem, in the house of the LORD, before the new court, 6And said, O LORD God of our fathers, art not thou God in heaven? and rulest not thou over all the kingdoms of the heathen? and in thine hand is there not power and might, so that none is able to withstand thee? 7Art not thou our God, who didst drive out the inhabitants of this land before thy people Israel, and gavest it to the seed of Abraham thy friend for ever? {who: Heb. thou} 8 And they dwelt therein, and have built thee a sanctuary therein for thy name, saying, 9 If, when evil cometh upon us, as the sword, judgment, or pestilence, or famine, we stand before this house, and in thy presence, (for thy name is in this house,) and cry unto thee in our affliction, then thou wilt hear and help. 10 And now, behold, the children of Ammon and Moab and mount Seir, whom thou wouldest not let Israel invade, when they came out of the land of Egypt, but they turned from them, and destroyed them not; 11 Behold, I say, how they reward us, to come to cast us out of thy possession, which thou hast given us to inherit. 12 O our God, wilt thou not judge them? for we have no might against this great company that cometh against us; neither know we what to do: but our eyes are upon thee. 13 And all Judah stood before the LORD, with their little ones, their wives, and their children. 14 Then upon Jahaziel the son of Zechariah, the son of Benaiah, the son of Jeiel, the son of Mattaniah, a Levite of the sons of Asaph, came the Spirit of the LORD in the midst of the congregation; 15And he said, Hearken ye, all Judah, and ye inhabitants of Jerusalem, and thou king Jehoshaphat, Thus saith the LORD unto you, Be not afraid nor dismayed by reason of this great multitude; for the battle is not yours, but God's. 16To morrow go ye down against them: behold, they come up by the cliff of Ziz; and ye shall find them at the end of the brook, before the wilderness of Jeruel. {cliff: Heb. ascent} {brook: or, valley} 17Ye shall not need to fight in this battle: set yourselves, stand ye still, and see the salvation of the LORD with you, O Judah and Jerusalem: fear not, nor be dismayed; to morrow go out against them: for the LORD will be with you. 18And Jehoshaphat bowed his head with his face to the ground: and all Judah and the inhabitants of Jerusalem fell before the LORD, worshipping the LORD. 19And the Levites, of the children of the Kohathites, and of the children of the Korhites, stood up to praise the LORD God of Israel with a loud voice on high.20And they rose early in the morning, and went forth into the wilderness of Tekoa: and as they went forth, Jehoshaphat stood and said, Hear me, O Judah, and ye inhabitants of Jerusalem; Believe in the LORD your God, so shall ye be established; believe his prophets, so shall ye prosper. 21And when he had consulted with the people, he appointed singers unto the LORD, and that should praise the beauty of holiness, as they went out before the army, and to say, Praise the LORD; for his mercy endureth for ever. {that...: Heb. praisers} 22And when they began to sing and to praise, the LORD set ambushments against the children of Ammon, Moab, and mount Seir, which were come against Judah; and they were smitten. {And when...: Heb. And in the time that they, etc} {to sing...: Heb. in singing and praise} {they were...: or, they smote one another} 23For the children of Ammon and Moab stood up against the inhabitants of mount Seir, utterly to slay and destroy them: and when they had made an end of the inhabitants of Seir, every one helped to destroy another. {to destroy: Heb. for the destruction} 24And when Judah came toward the watch tower in the wilderness, they looked unto the multitude, and, behold, they were dead bodies fallen to the earth, and none escaped. {none...: Heb. there was not an escaping} 25And when Jehoshaphat and his people came to take away the spoil of them, they found among them in abundance both riches with the dead bodies, and precious jewels, which they stripped off for themselves, more than they could carry away: and they were three days in gathering of the spoil, it was so much. 26And on the fourth day they assembled themselves in the valley of Berachah; for there they blessed the LORD: therefore the name of the same place was called, The valley of Berachah, unto this day. {Berachah: that is, blessing} 27Then they returned, every man of Judah and Jerusalem, and Jehoshaphat in the forefront of them, to go again to Jerusalem with joy; for the LORD had made them to rejoice over their enemies. {forefront: Heb. head} 28And they came to Jerusalem with psalteries and harps and trumpets unto the house of the LORD. 29And the fear of God was on all the kingdoms of those countries, when they had heard that the LORD fought against the enemies of Israel. 30So the realm of Jehoshaphat was quiet: for his God gave him rest round about.31And Jehoshaphat reigned over Judah: he was thirty and five years old when he began to reign, and he reigned twenty and five years in Jerusalem. And his mother's name was Azubah the daughter of Shilhi. 32And he walked in the way of Asa his father, and departed not from it, doing that which was right in the sight of the LORD. 33Howbeit the high places were not taken away: for as yet the people had not prepared their hearts unto the God of their fathers. 34Now the rest of the acts of Jehoshaphat, first and last, behold, they are written in the book of Jehu the son of Hanani, who is mentioned in the book of the kings of Israel. {book of Jehu: Heb. words, etc} {is mentioned: Heb. was made to ascend} 35And after this did Jehoshaphat king of Judah join himself with Ahaziah king of Israel, who did very wickedly: 36And he joined himself with him to make ships to go to Tarshish: and they made the ships in Eziongeber. 37Then Eliezer the son of Dodavah of Mareshah prophesied against Jehoshaphat, saying, Because thou hast joined thyself with Ahaziah, the LORD hath broken thy works. And the ships were broken, that they were not able to go to Tarshish.

God used praise and worship in many ways and He is still using it in our time. The Lord is calling for true worshippers that will worship Him in the Spirit and in truth. He desires for His praise to be in their mouths as a double edged sword, even as a kind of strength that comes from their mouths in this age.

The Lamb of God must be worshipped.

Revelation 5.1-14 *And I saw in the right hand of him that sat on the throne a book written within and on the backside, sealed with seven seals. 2 And I saw a strong angel proclaiming with a loud voice, Who is worthy to open the book, and to loose the seals* *thereof? 3 And no man in heaven, nor in earth, neither under the earth, was able to open the book, neither to look thereon. 4 And I wept much, because no man was found worthy to open and to read the book, neither to look thereon. 5 And one of the elders saith unto me, Weep not: behold, the Lion of the tribe of Juda, the Root of David, hath prevailed to open the book, and to loose the seven seals thereof.6 And I beheld, and, lo, in the midst of the throne and of the four beasts, and in the midst of the elders, stood a Lamb as it had been slain, having seven horns and seven eyes, which are the seven Spirits of God sent forth into all the earth. 7 And he came and took the book out of the right hand of him that sat upon the throne. 8 And when he had taken the book, the four beasts and four and twenty elders fell down before the Lamb, having every one of them harps, and golden vials full of odours, which are the prayers of saints. {odours: or, incense} 9 And they sung a new song, saying, Thou art worthy to take the book, and to open the seals thereof: for thou wast slain, and hast redeemed us to God by thy blood out of every kindred, and tongue, and people, and nation; 10 And hast made us unto our God kings and priests: and we shall reign on the earth. 11 And I beheld, and I heard the voice of many angels round about the throne and the beasts and the elders: and the number of them was ten thousand times ten thousand, and thousands of thousands; 12 Saying with a loud voice, Worthy is the Lamb that was slain to receive power, and riches, and wisdom, and strength, and honour, and glory, and blessing. 13 And every creature which is in heaven, and on the earth, and under the earth, and*

In the world to come, we will continue to offer Him the fruit of our lips. Friends, we must know that God deserves our true worship (worship that is done in spirit and in truth), and only true worshippers can dwell behind the veil (only they can enter into the Holy of Holies). Until He comes, continue to be a faithful and true worshipper.

Prayer of confession

If you have not confessed Christ as your Lord and Savior, you can do it now because today, if you hear His voice, do not harden your heart. It's your day.

Say this prayer.

Prayer

Lord Jesus, this hour I (*mention your name here*) confess you as my personal Savior and Lord. I now invite you to come into my life (my heart), take control over my life, and give me eternal life. Write my name in the Lamb's book of life; and help me Lord, to walk in the light of your word for the rest of my life, in Jesus' name I pray, Amen. (Rom 3:23, Rom 6:26, Rom 10:9-11)

Other works by Bishop Dr. Emmanuel Apau Jr.

1. The True Worshipper's Guide to His Presence

2. Seminar Handbook for Music Ministry

3. Touching God's Heart Through Prayer

4. The School of Joseph

5. Understanding Spiritual Gates and Doors

6. Church Planting and Evangelism

7. Demonology and Breaking of Curses

8. Godly Leadership and Management

9. Daily Devotional for Practical Ministry- Fresh Manna Vols. 1 &2

10. Ministry Leadership & Organization Structures

FIVE IMPORTANT QUESTIONS AND ANSWERS

1. Why do you and I need a savior?

Ans: Because everyone has sinned (Rom 3:23).

2. What is the result of sin?

Ans: The wages of sin is death (Both physical and spiritual) (Rom 6:23).

3. In what name can you and I be saved?

Ans: The name of Jesus Christ (Acts 4:12).

4. How will you and I come back into God's original plan?

Ans: By believing in Christ Jesus, God's son (John 1:12).

5. What do we gain by accepting Christ as our savior and Lord?

Ans: Everlasting glory or eternal life (John 3: 16).